ISBN 978-1-334-47770-6
PIBN 10756183

This book is a reproduction of an important historical work. Forgotten Books uses
state-of-the-art technology to digitally reconstruct the work, preserving the original format
whilst repairing imperfections present in the aged copy. In rare cases, an imperfection in
the original, such as a blemish or missing page, may be replicated in our edition. We do,
however, repair the vast majority of imperfections successfully; any imperfections that
remain are intentionally left to preserve the state of such historical works.

English
Français
Deutsche
Italiano
Español
Português

www.forgottenbooks.com

Mythology Photography **Fiction**
Fishing Christianity **Art** Cooking
Essays Buddhism Freemasonry
Medicine **Biology** Music **Ancient
Egypt** Evolution Carpentry Physics
Dance Geology **Mathematics** Fitness
Shakespeare **Folklore** Yoga Marketing
Confidence Immortality Biographies
Poetry **Psychology** Witchcraft
Electronics Chemistry History **Law**
Accounting **Philosophy** Anthropology
Alchemy Drama Quantum Mechanics
Atheism Sexual Health **Ancient History**
Entrepreneurship Languages Sport
Paleontology Needlework Islam
Metaphysics Investment Archaeology
Parenting Statistics Criminology
Motivational

THE

SONS OF GODWIN.

A TRAGEDY.

BY

WILLIAM LEIGHTON, Jr.

"There's a divinity that shapes our ends,
Rough-hew them how we will."

PHILADELPHIA:

J. B. LIPPINCOTT & CO.

1877.

DRAMATIS PERSONÆ.

———◦◦◦———

EDWARD THE THIRD, of the Saxon line, King of England.

HARALD HARDRADA, King of Norway.

EARL HAROLD, afterward king,
EARL TOSTIG, } Sons of Godwin.
EARL GURTH,

EARL MORKAR.

ALDRED, Archbishop of York.

STIGAND, Archbishop of Canterbury.

GUTHLAC, a thane.

MOLLO, a minstrel.

OSBALD, a messenger.

HUGH MARGOT, a Norman priest.

SEXWULF, a Saxon slave.

Messengers from Exeter, Sandwich, and Hastings.

Thanes, priests, English soldiers, Norwegian soldiers, attendants, guards, servants, etc.

THE COUNTESS GYTHA, widow of Earl Godwin.

THE LADY EDITH.

An Abbess.

Saxon women.

————————

Time of the drama, A.D. 1065–6.

2062129

THE SONS OF GODWIN.

THE SONS OF GODWIN.

ACT I.

SCENE I.—LONDON.

An antechamber in the house of EARL HAROLD.

GUTHLAC *and* MOLLO.

MOLLO.

Most noble thane, I would not push myself,
So well I know my insignificance,
Into your thoughts, but that I plainly see
In the dark sombreness of your grave face,
The fitful flashing of your eagle eye,
The furious champing of your long moustache,
That weighty matter fills your valiant breast;
And though a gleeman I, unknown to fame,
I fain would find some grand and swelling theme
On which my song may soar to fame's renown;
For, little as I am, I sigh for fame,
The poet's fame, the glory of the bard;

So, mighty Guthlac, let me have your thought,
That both may live heroic through all time,
The poet-minstrel and the warrior-thane.

GUTHLAC.

A saucy laugher, naming thus yourself,
Although ceorl-born, before you name a thane—
Despite your folly and your laughing sneers,
The stuff my thought is made of might indeed
Yield to the minstrel fitting theme of song:
I thought of Gryffyth, Cymry's dragon-king,
Whom late we tracked to his wild mountain crags,
And brought to bay where eagle aeries perch,
Bathed in the moisture of the floating clouds.

MOLLO.

O aye; you were with Harold in his wars,
And leaped like Welsh goat on steep Penmaen-mawr;
I bow to the brave hero, whose great shouts
Frighted the eagles from their Cymrian cliffs.

GUTHLAC.

Scoffer, brave fight the gallant Welsh king made,
And died at bay, as dies the mountain bear,
Destroying his destroyers.   Our great earl,
Victor alike on sea, on lowland plain,

Or high in air among the cloudy cliffs,
Wise as Earl Godwin, and as Tostig brave,
Himself declared, though England's weal required
The Welshman's death, his grand heroic end
In festal halls should England's minstrels sing.

MOLLO.

List while I frame my verse to this great theme;
Inspired by Polyhymnia I will sing.

> *To the music of his harp* MOLLO *chants the fol-*
> *lowing verses :*

Penmaen-mawr is tinged with blue,
Gleaming in the sky's bright hue,
Piercing mists and cloudlets through,
            Vastly grand.

Shouts resound amid the skies;
Craggy cliffs reflect wild cries;
Shrieking, loud an eagle flies
            Far away;

What affrights the feathered king?
What alarums loudly ring
Round the crags while banners fling
            Wide their folds?

A*

See the spear-points shining bright;
On broad axe-heads gleams the light;
Harold climbs with Saxon might
         Cymry's hold.

In the wildest spot of all,
Highest peak of mountains tall,
Rugged rocks, his fortress-wall,
         Gryffyth stands.

Once his race possessed the land,
Valleys, plains and mountains grand;
To the sea on either hand
         All was theirs.

First the conquering Roman came;
Then the spoiling Pict and Dane;
Last the Saxon from the main
         Landed here.

Robbed of all his wide domains,
Driven from fair vales and plains,
Naught of all to him remains
         But these crags.

Yes, he has his freedom still,
Dauntless heart and iron will
Never servile place to fill;
         These are his.

As they track the savage bear
Growling to his mountain lair,
Hedge him round and slay him there,
    Gryffyth fell.

Let the bards his story tell:
How a British hero fell,
He, whom Death alone could quell,
    Gryffyth brave.

GUTHLAC.

'Twas a brave end; but this is not the song
Your minstrelsy should raise in Harold's halls—
Harold, the vanquisher of Cymry's king;
Such poesy will bring you no reward
Unless you sing it on high Penmaen-mawr,
Where some poor Welshman, passion-stirred by it,
May bind your brow with odoriferous leeks.
A servant of this house should bid his muse
Sing not the death-songs of retreating kings,
But the bold music of advancing chiefs,
Of Brythnoth, slayer of the Danish jarl,
Of sea-king Wulfnoth, the brave Childe of Sussex,
Of Godwin, father of a mighty race,
Of Harold, guardian genius of the land,
Of Tostig, fearing neither man nor fiend,

Of Leofwine who laughs amid the battle,
Of Gurth, the true—

MOLLO.

Of Guthlac, poet-warrior.

GUTHLAC.

Nay, minstrel: these great names on flood of song
Will grandly sail far down the stream of Time,
Awakening echoes on its sounding shores
When such as yours and mine forgotten sleep.

MOLLO.

You should have been a minstrel.

GUTHLAC.
                    Yes, perhaps.

MOLLO.

I took my theme of Gryffyth from your lips.

GUTHLAC.

Then 'twas the poet, not the soldier, spoke.
Pshaw! Saxon and Cymrian—'tis to match
A kingly lion with a mountain cat,
An eagle with a kite—

Enter EARL GURTH.

Welcome, my Lord.

GURTH.

Fair greeting to you, brave and honest Guthlac.
My brother—is he here?

GUTHLAC.

He is, my Lord—
Pardon; I see grave import in your face:
If you have news from court that may be told
To one who hath the English weal at heart,
To one, the leal adherent of your house,
I ask your tidings.

GURTH.

None more leal than Guthlac.
Yet this same news that makes my features grave,
Event of import to all Englishmen,
Is common property to every ear:
Edward the Ætheling to-day is dead.

Exit EARL GURTH *across.*

GUTHLAC.

The Ætheling dead!

MOLLO.

You do purse up your lips,
Great Guthlac; is it sorrow?

GUTHLAC.

Nay indeed,
Not sorrow.   Though a prince of Cerdic's line,
And son of valiant Edmund Ironside,
True Saxon hero and brave English king,
Yet this dead Ætheling was not a hero.
While yet a child King Canute banished him,
And thus he ever lived a foreign man,
Until, advanced in years, our king recalled,
And purposed making him the kingdom's heir:
A purpose thwarted by the King of kings,
That England's ruler, when Saint Edward dies,
May be a hero and true Englishman,
To guard the soil, and drive the Norman forth,
A Saxon monarch though not Cerdic's line.

MOLIO.

Amen to that, all Saxon England cries,
Ealdorman, thane, the ceorl, even the slave—
And I, a gleeman.

Enter SEXWULF, *who bows awkwardly to* GUTHLAC.

GUTHLAC.

Wherefore come you here?

SEXWULF.

Most noble Sir, it is to see the Earl.

MOLLO, *bowing very low.*

Rest you well, fair Sir.

SEXWULF, *bowing stiffly.*

And you. (*Aside.*) It is a gleeman.

MOLLO.

Great Guthlac, you are king unto this Sir;
Lo! how he scorns the gleeman! all unmindful
That poesy hath power to lift a minstrel
Up to the level of a line of kings.

GUTHLAC.

Or folly hath. (*To* SEXWULF.) Know you, Sir Knave,
     the Earl
Grants not his audience to every theow.

SEXWULF.

Most noble Sir, I pray you give me leave—
> SEXWULF *comes close to* GUTHLAC, *shows him a
> letter secretly, and whispers.*

Greeting from Lady Edith to Earl Harold.

GUTHLAC (*aside*).

A most rude envoy from a most fair lady.

MOLLO.

Are you indeed an Earl in low disguise,
That noble Guthlac listens to your whisper?

GUTHLAC.

Beware, Sir Gleeman! with the Earl you trifle,
Daring to trifle with his messenger.

MOLLO, *bowing to* SEXWULF.

I humbly bow to Greatness in disguise.

GUTHLAC.

Follow me, theow; Earl Gurth is with my Lord,
And by-and-by you shall have audience.
> *Exeunt,* MOLLO *still bowing with mock solemnity
> to* SEXWULF.

SCENE II.—LONDON.

An apartment in the house of EARL HAROLD. *A table with papers, maps, plans, etc.*

EARL HAROLD *and* EARL GURTH.

GURTH.

It seems but yesterday, though five months past,
When, with the honors due his high descent,
We welcomed home this son of Ironside.
With eager eyes I scanned his features o'er,
The face of him who might be England's king,
To mark if Nature's kingly stamp were there.
I looked in vain for aught of majesty;
A weak, pale, anxious, sad, dejected face.
I heard his querulous voice impatient ask, .
How long the ceremonial of reception
And all the tedious formúlaries would last;
He came not like a monarch to his realm,
But as a sick man to a hospital;
Then well I knew that narrow brow too weak
To hold the dignity of England's crown;
Beneath such feeble rule as his had been,
England's broad bosom had been torn with broils;

B   2*

Nor even Harold's steadfast arm and brain
Kept the weak sceptre of such languid king
From trailing in the dust.   His timely death,
Clearing the pathway for a better king,
Will save the realm much ruinous disorder,
Although for England fails great Cerdic's line.

HAROLD.

His son yet lives, the heir to England's throne.

GURTH.

Edgar the Ætheling is but a boy,
Too young and much too feeble in his mind
To bear the burden of our island-crown.

HAROLD.

Yet he is heir by lineal descent.

GURTH.

Nay, Harold, not alone by lineage
Do England's kings possess the regal crown:
Fitness to rule, the people's confidence,
Choice in the council of the ealdormen,
Concurring, give a ruler to the state.
Edward the Elder, dying, left two sons,
Edmund and Edred, both legitimate;

Yet, by a choice in the witena-gemot given,
The bastard Æthelstan received the crown :
He was succeeded by his lawful heir ;
But after Edmund, Edred was the king,
Passing the claims of Edwin, Edmund's son.

HAROLD.

'Tis true that custom hath passed by such heirs,
And England's ealdormen can make a king.

GURTH.

Brother, the king grows weaker, mind and hand ;
Day after day his vital force is sapped ;
Nor all the relics of the blessed saints,
Gathered from far and near at England's cost
By our saint-king, can work the miracle
To far prolong his life : and England sees
The end approaching of this monarch's reign ;
The end approaching of this kingly line ;
And rests content : nor dreads the Norman Duke,
Nor fears the war-ships of the Danish king—
And why content ? Because the people look
To you, my brother, at King Edward's death
To hold secure and firm the English state.
Our present monarch is a thing of form ;
All are content to yield him majesty,

But look to you when England needs a king
For the strong arm to battle with her foes,
The prudent head to frame fit policy.

HAROLD.

If I might better serve my native land
By placing on this young boy's brow the crown,
As our wise father crowned the present king,
No vain ambition would prevent, nor lust
Of royal state make me usurp his place.

GURTH.

The choice is not with you ; the ealdormen
Will never crown this youthful Ætheling.
The realm of England—shall it be a pawn
To play and lose for such a king as he ;
A child to play it too ?   At Edward's death
To you must come the proffer of the crown ;
The Saxons know you as the wisest son
Of great Earl Godwin ; Danes remember you
Descended through our mother from a line
Of Danish sea-kings ; Saxons, Danes, alike
Throughout all England, see no other chief
Than Harold, skilled to lead by land or sea,
Whose arms adventurous ne'er have known defeat :

No Englishman like him, dear to the hearts
Of all, thane-born or lowly ceorl.

HAROLD.

O Gurth,
I never felt our father's death as now.
Would he were still alive to wear this crown !
How proudly we, his sons, would stand by him,
Buttress his throne with faithful hearts and hands,
Making fair England the most prosperous land
Beneath the sky !   His careful policy,
Our arms victorious, borne by fame abroad,
Had scared invasion from our guarded shores.

GURTH.

Harold, our father lives again in you ;
You have his wisdom, valor, and inherit
All the renown they yielded in his life ;
You have beyond our father England's love,
And, as he had the duty of his sons,
You have the constant love and faithful service
Of Gurth and Leofwine, although, alas !
Little they bring you but devoted love.

HAROLD.

Never had man two wiser, braver brothers,

Dear Gurth, than you and Leofwine.   Alone
I could not hope, as now, to make safe way
In camp and court through all impediment.
Certain, amid the slippery faiths of men,
That two are sure, I have a triple strength.

GURTH.

Our hearts and acts are yours; you are the head,
And we the limbs, the servants of its will.
You will be king; our father, ere he died,
Foresaw the English crown upon your head,
And bade your brothers be leal men to you,
Head of our house and of the English realm.
Our banished Sweyn is lost to you and England;
Wolnoth, a hostage with the Norman Duke;
Tostig, an erring slave of his own passions;
But Leofwine is true, and Gurth is leal.

HAROLD.

My faithful Gurth! but naming Sweyn and Tostig
Calls up a sorrow heavy in my heart;
Sweyn's fate is sealed; an irrevocable shame,
Alas! blots out his name; Tostig, I fear,
Will err as rashly, and as sadly fall:
He has no thought for England, all for self;
His earldom but the means to gratify

Passion, self-glory, a licentious will
That grasps at all.   Pray Heaven it send to him
A better angel to defeat the fiends
That battle for his soul !

GURTH.

Our brother Wolnoth, long detained at Rouen
Against the king's request and frequent message,
Is his fond mother's grief; with tearful eyes
She questions every Norman messenger
For news of him.   May we not find the means
To win her darling back to her once more?

HAROLD.

Wolnoth at Rouen holds anomalous place.
As hostage for his father's plighted faith
With our King Edward, sent to Normandy
Because Earl Godwin was all-powerful here,
And Norman William, Edward's friend and cousin,
Our father's death should have set free his pledge ;
But William's policy retains him still, .
In guise of friendship, but in fact a check
Upon his kinsmen, none the less a hostage
Because he seems a favorite of the Duke,
And held in silken bonds.

Enter GUTHLAC, *ushering the* LADY GYTHA.

GUTHLAC.

The Lady Gytha.

Exit GUTHLAC.

HAROLD.

My mother—

GURTH.

My dear mother—

GYTHA.

Harold, my son,
Pride of our house.

GURTH.

And what am I, dear mother?

GYTHA.

No less than Harold your fond mother's pride.

HAROLD.

But your attendants, mother, where are they ;
A sea-king's daughter goes not unattended?

GYTHA.

I bade them wait me in the antechamber.

HAROLD.

Pray, mother, sit.

GYTHA.

Nay, Harold, not as guest, but suppliant,
I come to you.   Oh, see me on my knees.

HAROLD, *raising* GYTHA.

My mother, rise ; nor kneel unto your son,
Whose place is at your feet, not you at his.

GYTHA.

Harold, my widowed heart is full of grief.
· No English mother hath such sons as mine,
Then why should I be sad?   Your glory, Harold,
Is dear to me as was your father's fame ;
Above all Englishmen my Harold towers,
And soon, I know, his head will wear a crown ;
Gurth, Leofwine and Tostig all are earls ;
But Wolnoth, ah ! is exiled from his land
And from his mother's arms.   O Harold, Gurth,
I think of you, and swells my heart with pride,
Of Wolnoth, and my pride is drowned in tears ;
Why are you placed so high, and he exiled?

B   3

HAROLD.

Mother, you know how oft at my request
The king hath sent to call my brother back.

GYTHA.

Harold, in England what you will is law,
The monk-king's sceptre but a gilded toy;
Had you your mother's heart you would reclaim,
Despite refusal, my long-exiled son,
Thus held from his ancestral place and honors,
From home and arms of fond, maternal love.
His father's death should have set free my boy.
Hath he no brothers, that he pines in chains?
Or is a Norman Duke too high to question?

GURTH.

Mother, the Duke in Normandy is king,
And Wolnoth wears no chains.

GYTHA.

                 Gurth, iron gyves
May gall the limbs, but fettered liberty
Chafes inwardly. Wolnoth may wear the smile
That lighted up the face of Sparta's boy
When the fox ate his heart. My friendless son!

Thus would your mother act were she Earl Harold :
Send the war-arrows over all the land,
Launch the long war-ships, cross the narrow seas,
And rouse Duke William in his Norman court
With the bold music of your sea-king sires.

HAROLD.

Now speaks the fiery blood of bearded jarls ;
Mother, you are true daughter of the Dane.

GYTHA.

O Harold, I have waited year on year
And bade my heart be still, for he would come,
At last would come unto my longing arms ;
But the years pass, and yet he doth not come,
And still I strive to wait most patiently,
Till patience dies within my aching heart ;
And now I come to ask my kingly son
To give his mother back her exiled son.
My Harold, you are wise ; o'er all the land
Your wisdom and your valor are the shield,
And England sleeps secure beneath its ægis.
The wretched ceorl seeks from you redress
Of wrong or scath ; your wisdom and your power
Pluck down oppression, give him back his own ;
Your mother seeks redress for a great wrong :

Her child is kept from her maternal breast.
Shall the base peasant have your ready aid,
And not your mother? Give me Wolnoth, Harold;
She asks you this who gave to you your life,
And, with your life, your wisdom and your valor.

HAROLD.

My mother, all I am and have is yours;
To win back Wolnoth I would give my life.

GYTHA.

Ah no, son Harold! though my bosom aches
To clasp to it my youngest child again,
Yet never let me see my darling more
Sooner than purchase him by loss of you.
What I would have you do, is trust no more
To the vain hope that Edward's messengers
Can bring your brother to us; you must act:
How, your own wisdom is the safest guide,
Nor dare I offer counsel. Harold, promise
That this one thought, how to restore my son,
Shall have precedence of all other matter
And promptest execution in your acts.

HAROLD.

I promise it, my mother; and a project,

Often revolved and weighed within my mind,
Shall speedily set forward : I will go,
Not with my war-ships, but as peaceful guest,
And bring our Wolnoth from the Norman court.

GURTH.

You go to Normandy as William's guest !
I see not in this plan the wise foresight
Of shrewd Earl Godwin's son.

GYTHA.

      Placing yourself
Unhostaged in the power of this bold Norman
Will lose me both my sons.

HAROLD.

      I think not so ;
What would Duke William gain, retaining me ?
I am too great to keep me as a hostage,
And he hath two already ; nor my death
Would bring advantage to him ; I may win
His friendship, make alliance with his power.
Truly he hath the fame of courtesy,
And knightly honor is his darling theme,
Nor hath he object, nor could find excuse,
To stay or injure a confiding guest.

GURTH.

A firm alliance of our house with William
Hath show of wisdom in it; but 'tis bold
To test an untried magnanimity.

GYTHA.

I trust your wisdom, for you are not rash;
I trust your promise, for I know you, true;
And I shall have my Wolnoth.

HAROLD.

                Nay, my mother;
The fate of man is in the womb of .Time,
And rash is he who dares to say I will—
But the best efforts of my mind and hands
I promise you, to win my brother back,
Nor shall I now be idle.

GYTHA.

            Thanks, dear son.
Gurth, come with me. Am I not like a queen
When I have earls that kindly wait on me?

HAROLD.

Your blessing, mother. (*Kneels.*)

GYTHA.

Angels shield you, son,
To build yet higher your great father's house ;
To be the mighty warden of the land—
And give you happiness.

HAROLD.

Farewell, my mother,
Nor ever think me lukewarm in your cause.
Exeunt GYTHA *and* GURTH.

The Norman Duke hath gathered at his court
Learning and arts, the progress of the world ;
Whatever may be culled out of the past,
Or wrought by patient labor in the present.
In untrained nature slumber inert powers,
Waiting the hand of genius to bring forth
Their latent might ; or, lacking that, they grow
In the warm light of fair prosperity
As young plants grow.   One larger mind, advanced
Beyond the rest, may bring their progress on
As cultivation makes of languishing plants
A fruitful harvest.   Rumor fills my ears,
With every south wind, how Duke William builds
Stronger his state ; how artisan and soldier,
The troubadour with spirit-stirring songs,

The scholar with his rolls of parchment lore,
All find a welcome at his court, and each
A patient pupil in this famous Duke;
While all their several arts he welds together
Into new forms of power to strengthen him.
The Pyrrhic phalanx and the Roman legion
Afford him studies; to their art he adds
New forms of discipline, till joined as one,
And animate with but a single thought,
His army moves; the single thought his own.
His skillful artisans have fashioned arms
With curious craft, and practice betters them.
What have we here to match him, if perchance
He deems his cousinship deserves a throne?
Our Englishmen have courage, little skill,
No patient training in the arts of war;
We fight as fought our sires of long ago,
With the same weapons and rude forms of war.
The Roman crushed the Briton, brave as he,
By force of discipline and better arms;
Our Saxon fathers won this English soil
Because more practiced and inured to war
Than peaceful villagers grown dull by sloth;
And now the Norman, trained in martial skill,
May overmatch the stronger Englishman
If England slothful sleeps.   Valor and strength

Will arm the Saxon hero's hand in vain
If he must fight at every disadvantage
And fall by strategy.   Valor and strength
Are simply brutal parts; the lion claims
His kingly share of these, but yields to man
His savage life when the sharp javelin
Or flying arrow pierces his great heart,
And intellect is victor over strength.
Duke William's power is brain.   To Normandy,
Thus called, I must perforce adventure me;
See all the wonders bruited over seas;
Study the master-spirit of the land;
Win him, if possible, for England's friend:
Or, failing this, returned again with Wolnoth,
Train English armies into Norman skill.   *Exit.*

B*   C

SCENE III.—LONDON.

The house of the LADY EDITH.

Enter EDITH *and* EARL HAROLD.

EDITH.

My Lord, I thank you for remembering
Our distant kinship, thus at once to answer
My hasty message.

HAROLD.

        Do not say our kinship—
Edith, it is remembrance of our kinship,
Although that kindred be a distant one,
And cousinship through two removes of blood,
That ever haunts me, shining in your eyes,
Staying the words unuttered on my lips.

EDITH.

My Lord, you speak impatiently and strange.

HAROLD.

Say not "My Lord," but, as of old time, "Harold."

EDITH.

You have become so mighty now, an earl,
And highest in the land; I scarcely dare
Remember how we were such friends of old
That then 'twas Cousin Harold.

HAROLD.

Harold ever
Let me remain unchanged in your remembrance,
As in delightful days of merry youth,
When our blithe hearts knew not that in this life
Shadows might come between us and our joys.

EDITH.

When I recall those pleasures, Cousin Harold,
And the companionship of those old days,
How gently and how nobly you would share
My girlish fancies, I am proud indeed
England hath set you in such high estate.

HAROLD.

Still "cousin—cousin;" Edith, I hate the word!

EDITH.

Hate the relationship that makes me proud?

HAROLD.

Edith, I love you as a wife, not cousin,
And the church bans and interdicts such marriage.
I long have struggled to repress my love,
And closely shut my lips when my wild words
Would have poured out the passion of my heart,
Because such love might be a thing accursed
By mitred prelates of our scrupulous church;
But in my heart the passion hath so grown
That I am powerless to restrain its floods,
And needs must tell you, Edith, of my love.
'Tis not unholy, such true love as mine,
However frowns on it the holy church;
For the church grants indulgencies ofttimes
By which such interdiction is removed:
On the which hope I rest my happiness,
Although King Edward, in his pious zeal,
May long withhold consent that we may wed.
I had resolved my love should be untold
Until such time as brighter promise dawned;
But now, departing from you and from England,
My heart breaks thus the silence of my lips.

EDITH.

Departing! Why and whither do you go?

HAROLD.

To Normandy.   My foremost purpose is
To claim the hostages my father gave
So long ago, his pledge of faith to Edward.
I go as guest to Norman William's court;
And though I think my visit brings no peril,
Yet many anxious cares oppress my breast,
Not cares for self, but for the realm of England;
While o'er my mind float strange, foreboding thoughts
And vague presentiments of coming evil.
Thus, with my heart o'erclouded, I have dared
To utter, Edith, words so long repressed,
To tell the hopes I cherish.   If your love,
Pledged to my heart, can go, my heart's companion,
With me from England, I shall go all blithely,
Ready to grapple the worst forms of evil
That can arise to menace me or England;
And the clouds moving darkly o'er my mind
Will be o'erspanned by Love's bright rainbow-arch.
Edith, your answer; is my hope in vain?

EDITH.

Nay, not in vain.

HAROLD.

So I have dared believe;
For love is watchful of the smallest things,

4

And finds a language in each look and smile,
Motion and act; the pensive, downcast eye,
The ringing laugh, are words that may be read
By harmless sorcery of anxious love—
A cipher-language, telling of the heart,
How its pulsations beat, while joy or pain
Writes its quick legend on the changeful brow.

EDITH.

I did not know my heart had been thus read,
But since its childhood it has beat for you;
And while you grew to greater fame and honor,
It still kept pace, and loved you more and more;
Not for your glory or illustrious name,
Both dear to me, nor that your kingly heart
And intellect, expressed in generous acts,
Have set you o'er our people; this would be
Fit cause for admiration and respect,
Not for such love as mine.   My childhood's friend,
Whose gentle hand gave ever-ready help,
Whose thoughtful eyes looked heartfelt sympathies,
Is dearest memory.   That holy church
Should place the cross between your heart and mine,
Was never in my thought.   If barred from you
By ban and interdiction, all my heart
Is yours, and my most fervent prayers arise
Daily to heaven to give you happy fortune.

HAROLD.

No fortune happy if it give not you—
I cannot say my heart is yours alone;
Edith, my heart is plighted from my youth
To England; but no less its wealth of love
For you that England shares with you its love.

EDITH.

And I might love you less if less your love
And grand devotion to your native land;
Throughout our country, when I look around,
Earls, chiefs, and thanes are struggling each for self,
All for aggrandizement of wealth or power.
Alone,of all, I see you still intent
On England's good, while even your father's sons
Are not like you, dear Harold, thus inspired.
Your brother Tostig—I am grieved to cast
A shadow on you when I should bring cheer—

HAROLD.

Speak, Edith; past experience hath schooled me
To hear ill news of misdirected Tostig.

EDITH.

Do you remember Cuthbert, Gunna's son?—

Gunna, my Danish nurse, who filled my mind,
In infancy, with all her wondrous lore
Of fierce exploits of jarl and viking wild,
The frightful terrors of the weird wolf-witch,
The dread scin-læca over warriors' tombs—
Cuthbert was long ago your playmate too;
Do you remember him?

HAROLD.

Yes, Edith, well;
Those pleasant years are stamped indelible
Upon my heart in happy memories.
If I can serve your Cuthbert, serving you
In this, I serve myself as well as you.

EDITH.

Our Cuthbert served Northumbria's great Earl,
Old famous Siward, whom your brother, Tostig,
Succeeded in his earldom.   Cuthbert loves
A virtuous lady of your brother's court,
Elgiva, in attendance on the Countess,
Betrothed to Cuthbert, though of higher birth.
Your brother, envying poor Cuthbert's favor,
Where, it is said, his lawless fancy fell,
Taunted my foster-brother with his birth
Until he drove him to some sharp reply,

Then banished him his court.   He sent to me,—
His letter brought by Sexwulf, a rude theow,—
Asking my intercession with Earl Harold,
To whom all England looks for equity,
To cure his sad, his most disastrous fortunes,
Too desperate, I fear, for a safe cure,
For, when I questioned this rude Sexwulf further,
I learned Earl Tostig's men were full in chase,
Hunting my foster-brother to his death.

HAROLD.

This is bad news, and comes perhaps too late.
My messenger shall go at once to Tostig,
And I will send a troop in search of Cuthbert;
If he yet live, my friendship shall be his,
To smooth, if possible, his path of love,
And give him his betrothed.

EDITH.

     So ever speaks
Your generous, kingly heart.   But do not stay;
A single moment may lose Cuthbert's life—
I must not stop you even with my thanks.

       Enter an attendant.

ATTENDANT.

A gentleman seeks audience of the Earl
With message from the king.

HAROLD.

Who is it?

ATTENDANT.

Guthlac.

HAROLD.

I'll see him presently.

Exit attendant.

My trustiest thane
Is Guthlac, and some urgent business calls
That thus he seeks me here.   Dear Edith, thanks,
My full heart's thanks, that you have cheered my heart
With your bright sun of love.   Whatever fate
Hath in abeyance for me, fair or foul,
Still greater honors or the loss of all,
My one great happiness must be your love.
If the near future hath for me a crown,
Which an ambitious eye would surely see,
My proudest hour will be when England hails
My Edith as her queen.   Farewell.

Harold kisses Edith's hand, and exit.

EDITH.

The one great hope, the fond, the darling dream
Of all my life at length is realized ;
For Harold loves me.   *Exit.*

ACT II.

SCENE I.—LONDON.

An antechamber in the house of EARL HAROLD.   *Table,*
chairs, and bench.

MOLLO *and* OSBALD.   SEXWULF *asleep on bench.*

MOLLO.

I pray you sit, and tell me more at length
By what strange chance Thane Gamel hath been slain
By Tostig's men; for so I caught the news
From Guthlac's words; and, if you love good ale,
Our cellarer shall send us here a brewage
Fit for a king.   Ho, Eric!
                    Enter a servant.
                              Bring us ale.
                                        Exit servant.

OSBALD, *sitting.*

Minstrel, in truth I am most sadly tired:
Two days and nights have brought no restful sleep,

But terror, anxious thought and weary travel—
The last twelve hours in saddle without rest—
This tires a man.　I'll try your vaunted ale;
In Nottingham we have a famous brewage.

MOLLO.

Not like the ale of Kent.　Their London ale
I will not boast of; but our Kentish ale,
Sweet, nut-brown ale, crowned like the king with pearl,
And frothy—as his butler.　Ah! my friend,
If Jove had tasted it, he had upset
His bowls of nectar, and sent Ganymede
To fetch him ale.　See yonder northern theow,
That slumbers on the bench; he found it good.

OSBALD.

Of Nottingham is he?

MOLLO.

Sexwulf his name;
He brought Earl Harold news out of the north,
And, as I think, owes service thereabout,
In Mercia, Nottingham—I cannot tell.
I thought to loose his sluggish tongue with ale,
Our Kentish ale; he gaped and swallowed it
As thirsty horse drinks water, but his tongue

Would only say the ale was very good ;
The stupid swine would tell me nothing more,
And soon fell fast asleep.

> *Enter servant with ale in a jug, which* MOLLO
> *pours and presents to* OSBALD.   *Exit servant.*

Try this, my friend,
And never drink your northern brewage more,
But sigh regretful for the ale of Kent.

OSBALD *drinks.*

'Tis good (*drinks*).   The ale is good (*drinks*).   Yes,
    very good.

MOLIO.

'Tis what that sleeper said before he slept ;
I trust the ale will not so tie your tongue .
But that you can deliver me the news
For which you sacrificed your two nights' sleep,
And took this long, and doubtless weary, ride.

OSBALD.

Weary indeed !   Right glad am I 'tis over ;
I safely housed, and drinking this good ale (*drinks*).

MOLLO.

" Good ale," is still what sleepy Sexwulf cried.

OSBALD.

Well, you shall have my story. 'Twas after midnight;
The household hushed in slumber most profound—

MOLLO.

What house, my friend?

OSBALD.

     Our house, Thane Gamel's house
In Nottingham, near Sherwood. All asleep;
When on the stillness broke the tramp of feet,
A horse's hoofs. It stops; then comes a knocking
Upon the great hall-door, locked for the night,
And fastened with a bar. This roused up all.
I know not how I scrambled to the hall,
But there were all the servants in alarm,
Not dressed, but each with pike, boar-spear, or axe,
Caught up in hurry to defend the house;
And there was our young thane, with his great sword
Naked in both his hands, but in his night-gown
Like all the rest; and still the noisy knocking
Hammered impatiently upon the door.
Some from the upper windows tried to look
Into the court below; but all was darkness
Under the shadow of the eastern wall.

Then Gamel gripped his sword, and stood in front,
And bade us draw the bar.   Those perched above
At the hall-windows shouted, "Keep the door!"
But Gamel, thinking that they cried in fear,
Bade us in haste to loose and swing it back;
So, drawing bolt and bar, we opened it:
When, from the darkness, sprang into the light
A man all travel-stained; on whose pale face
Was terror's frightful stamp.   We knew the man;
'Twas Cuthbert, a Northumbrian, who came
Sometimes to see our thane.

     SEXWULF, *who has awakened, listens very at-*
     tentively.

                             He seized the door
As if to swing it back, but was too late;
A throng of men, all armed, came pouring in—
Earl Tostig's men; I knew them by their badge,
A silver war-ship.   Cuthbert rushed to Gamel,
Crying, "They come to kill me; Gamel, help!"
Our fearless thane, though thus surprised, stood fast,
Swung his great sword above his head, and cried,
"Back—back, Northumbrians; by my father's soul
Ye shall not have this man!"   But on they came,
And we were only twenty to a hundred,
Naked and scarcely armed.   A flash of swords;
Down went the foremost under Gamel's stroke,

But ere his arm could thrice repeat the blow
The hundred were upon him, and he fell ;
While, fighting by his side, was Cuthbert killed.

SEXWULF *comes forward.*

SEXWULF.

Was Cuthbert killed ?   Art sure they killed him too ?
He might be hurt and fall, but yet not killed—

OSBALD.

I saw them hack him with a hundred wounds,
Each one of which was mortal.   Who are you
That seem to take such interest in the man ?

SEXWULF.

Hacked with a hundred wounds ! Cuthbert is dead !

OSBALD.

Yes, surely dead.   But you—are you Northumbrian ?

SEXWULF.

He saved my life—I know not how to say it—
He saved the slave that others spurned in scorn ;
And the slave loved him—loved, as a dog loves,
Who, watchful of his master's smile or frown,
Takes joy or sorrow from the face he loves.

What now can Sexwulf do, but, like a dog,
Die on his grave? You said they cut and hacked him—
The cowards, murderers! Theow as I am,
I would have faced them, ceorl-born, thane-born,
Ay, Tostig's self, with axe, or pike, or spear,
Or with my naked hands, had I been there!

MOLLO.

Where did you leave him? Came you to the Earl
From this slain Cuthbert?

SEXWULF.

I came from north the Humber; came afoot;
Nor took much longer time than he on horse:
I ran in hope to save him, but he's dead—
Dead! dead! I am too late!

OSBALD.

               No fault of yours;
You had no time to save him, if the means.

MOLLO.

How could you give him help?

SEXWULF.

             I will not talk.
                Exit SEXWULF.

MOLLO.

This brutish theow has so marred your story
I know not yet how it hath chanced to you
To come so quickly here.

OSBALD.

                    The slave is rude ;
But, faith ! I cannot choose but pity him.
When I saw Gamel slain, in fear I fled ;
'Twas death to stay.   Through a side-door I passed ;
Ran through the house, familiar with the way,
And gained the stable, saddled a swift horse,
And rode into the night ; soon left behind
Death and the din of murder.   As I rode,
A lurid glow lit up the dismal night,
Tinting the dark skies with a crimson fire ;
Then, looking back, I saw long tongues of flame
Curling around the gables of our house,
And spurred my horse the faster.   To my heart
Now came wild terror, and my hair stood up ;
Cold drops of sweat were gathered on my brow ;
Dead Cuthbert's face, as when he crossed our door
With murderers behind him, haunted me
With its wild look of horror.   When at last
My mind grew calm, and when my heart no more
Thumped at my ribs, I fixed upon my course,

To seek Earl Morkar in Northamptonshire—
For Gamel was of·kindred to the Earl—
And bear him tidings of this midnight murder.
Morkar in silence heard me, stamped and frowned;
Then bade me take his letter to the king,
Nor slack my rein lest he be there before me.

MOLLO.

And the king sent you with your news to Harold?

OSBALD.

Unto Earl Harold, who is Tostig's brother;
And so it seems not clear to me how justice
Is likely to be dealt for my thane's murder
By your Earl's hands—

Enter GUTHLAC.

GUTHLAC *to* OSBALD.

    The Earl is waiting you.
    Exeunt GUTHLAC *and* OSBALD.

MOLLO.

This is the way Earl Tostig rules his earldom;
Hunting men down, and burning homes o' nights.
More promise for the soldier than the minstrel
I see in this. Heigh-ho! This bodes of war—

War, to despoil me of my comforts here,
Soft bed and Kentish ale. My wisest way
Is to enjoy them both while yet I may.

                Pours a stoop of ale, and drinks.

So now I'll go to bed.

                              Exit.

SCENE II.—LONDON.

Hall of state in the king's palace. The KING, EARLS
HAROLD, TOSTIG, GURTH, *and* MORKAR; ALDRED,
Archbishop of York; STIGAND, *Archbishop of Canterbury;* GUTHLAC; *thanes, guards, attendants, messengers, etc.*

FIRST MESSENGER.

Your Majesty,
Britwald, the ealdorman of Exeter,
True and leal servant unto England's king,
Sends to his king for aid. The pirate Rhud,
Round Cornwall sailing from the Irish seas,
With thirty long-ships hath besieged your town;
Threatening, unless a thousand pounds be paid,
His war-gild, to break down the city gates,

To seize its treasures as the spoils of war,
And set your servant's head upon a pike.

KING.

Earl Harold, how is this?   Two summers since
You swept these Irish pirates from the seas.
Who is this Rhud that dares besiege our town?

HAROLD.

My liege, these hornets swarm along the coasts
Of Ireland, Hebrides, and stormy Orkneys;
No broom can sweep them clean; among the isles
And thousand inlets of the Irish seas
They hide them, till some howling northern blast
May bring their swift ships to an English town:
From which they fly, oft laden with much spoil,
Ere we have time to strike a blow at them.

KING.

What may we do?   Shall we send out our ships
And raise the siege?   It surely is not wise
To pay these pirates war-gild.

HAROLD.

             Nay, my liege;
No money shall the bold forayers have.

Four days ago a message came to me
From the far north of this King Rhud's intent;
And instant Leofwine, my brother, sailed
With forty war-ships out of Medway frith;
Before whose keels the pirates have been driven
Back to their wild and stormy seas again,
Or King Rhud's head is set upon a pike.

KING.

My careful Harold l   England's weal is safe
Through the king's prayers and Harold's ready arm.

To Messenger.

The aid you ask for is already sent;
Go back and tell brave Britwald, England's arm
Is ever ready to protect our realm.

Exit Messenger.

Who is the second messenger that waits?

SECOND MESSENGER.

Your Majesty, I come from Sandwich's port,
Sent to the king by many citizens
Desiring that their sea-walls, greatly rent
By the late storms, be speedily repaired
And put in fit condition of defense.

Two weeks in London have I waited audience,
The while our walls are useless and o'erthrown ;
And had this Rhud sailed down the coast so far
He would have found our town without defense.

KING.

Harold, what answer shall we send to Sandwich ?
To build up sea-walls empties treasure-chests.
Our steward tells us that there is no money ;
He scarce could pay for that most precious relic,
Saint Peter's thumb.

ARCHBISHOP STIGAND.

My liege, a blessed relic ;
And safer guardian of our island shores
Than walls or war-ships !

HAROLD.

Doth your Reverence mean,
I might have saved my brother and his ships,
Sending a priest with Peter's thumb to Rhud?

ARCHBISHOP STIGAND.

The blessed relic would have scared the heathen,

HAROLD.

Perhaps; but Leofwine is sure to do it.

KING.

Harold, I grieve to hear such doubts from one
Whose life hath ever shown a noble mind.

ARCHBISHOP ALDRED *to* HAROLD.

More reverence unto holy church, my son,
Were more becoming to your high estate. ·

KING.

The messenger awaïts an answer, Harold,
Concerning Sandwich and its broken walls.

HAROLD *to Messenger.*

Your town itself should have rebuilt its walls.
Why do the lazy citizens thus wait,
And leave themselves defenseless?   It were well
King Rhud had paid his visit to your town,
A lesson that you need.   Return to Sandwich,
And tell the citizens that sent you hither,—
A graceless envoy from a slothful town,—
Unless their walls are up within three months
The king will levy a sufficient tax

On Sandwich to build up a mighty sea-wall,
Whose solid masonry will laugh at storms.
Begone ; and learn to wear more modest bearing
In presence of your king..   .

To attendants.

Take him away.

Exeunt attendants with messenger.

MORKAR.

My liege, I come before your throne to plead
For justice—simple justice.   Yours the rule
From Cornwall to the Tweed, and England owes
Unto your throne and crown its true allegiance ;
But what owe you to England as its king ?
You owe to all that life, goods, house and land,
The rights of ceorl, thane and ealdorman,
Shall be secure ; nor torn away by force,
By robber force, though wielded by an earl.
Lo ! here before your throne I take my stand ;
Claim from the king an Englishman's broad rights :
My cousin Gamel hath been basely murdered ;
His dwelling broken at the dead of night ;
His servants slain ; his house and goods despoiled,
And given up to fierce devouring flames,
By one who comes before your throne to-day

c*

Wearing the emblems of a belted earl.
I ask for justice.   Though his kindred stand
Highest around your throne, the laws of England
Require that punishment be dealt to crime.
I here demand the king shall take his earldom
From Tostig Godwinson, and that a witan
Sit on his acts.   If he be proven guiltless,
Then let him in Northumbria rule again ;
If guilty,—and his guilt is manifest,—
He is not fit to live on English soil.

TOSTIG.

And who are you—the censor of the realm—
To say this earl shall rule, and this shall not ?
What service unto England have you done ?
When the Welsh king rebelled against our liege
You fought on Gryffyth's side : but pardoned this
By clemency too lenient for such crime,
Yet still a traitor in your secret heart,
You would incite the king against his friends,
Whose swords cut off the head of your rebellion,
Because, forsooth, your cousin, harboring rebels,
Received the punishment was due to one.

MORKAR.

You taunt and fling at me a rebel's name ;

This thing is past.   Would you recall the past?
There is a legend current in the land
That once upon a time, my ancestor
Then Earl of Mercia, your much-boasted line
Sprang from a low-born cowherd.

TOSTIG.

It is false—
False as your lying lips.   My ancestor,
Brave Wulfnoth, was a nephew to the king;   .
And, though his youth was nursed in peasant's hut,
Proved his great ancestry by valiant acts
Worthy his lineage; and achieved a name,
"The Childe of Sussex," sung throughout the land
By minstrel lips to ears attuned to glory.
Your legend is most false.

MORKAR.

These boasts are naught.
I claim your punishment for lawless acts.

KING.

Earl Tostig, what have you to answer us
Upon this charge of outrage, midnight burning,
Murder?

TOSTIG.

My liege, in hot pursuit of one

Escaping justice, my officer and men
Came in the night through Sherwood's forest paths
To Nottingham; here, when they closed upon him,
The quarry won a refuge in the house
Of Gamel, son of Orm.   Against my men
Gamel opposed his household; in the tumult
The thane was killed, but not before he slew
Three of my men; for this they burned his house.

KING.

But Nottingham's in Mercia: wherefore, Earl,
Did you pursue the man beyond your earldom?

TOSTIG.

In the long chase across a country wide,
Who stops at night to mark dividing lines
And say "Here ends dominion of my Lord"?
I bade them take the man alive or dead;
And who was Gamel, that his hand should dare
To check the purpose of Northumbria's Earl?

KING.

Who was this criminal so fiercely sought?
A traitor to our crown? assassin? thief?
Surely his crimes had been of blackest dye,
Thus hunted down at night by your armed men?

TOSTIG.

And must an earl, allied to kings, bow down
Like a poor theow, and explain each act
Of justice done by him within his earldom?
The man was judged by me, his legal lord—
Judged, doomed, and had been executed too
Although he fled unto the farthest Orkney.

KING.

Storm not at us, Sir Earl; we know the story:
How you oppressed and injured this poor man
Because he murmured that you took his mate.
Oh, fie on you, a Christian earl, to steal,
And slay the victim to atone the theft!

TOSTIG.

Steals then the lion when in forests dark
He leaps upon his prey? or steals the eagle
When from his dizzy height he swiftly swoops
On frightened dove?   No, King; these do not steal.
They take by lordly power and right of might.
So, like a lion mid the beasts of field,
An eagle 'mong the birds, Earl Tostig rules
With men; and Nature gave him his fierce heart,
Strong arm and dauntless courage, as it gave
Tooth to the lion, talon to the eagle.

I steal, indeed!   By Hengist! if an earl,
A Saxon earl, have not so much of power
To rule his household, but must bend him low,
And answer every act to every neighbor
Who hath a cousin, you may give, O King,
Northumbria's earldom to this Morkar here,
This little earlling who is brave in talk;
And I will launch my war-ships, as of old
My fathers did; and, like the Childe of Sussex,
Mine ancestor, will reap my harvests where
Pale, trembling slaves are held in Law's base leash;
Myself a sea-king, and beyond all law.

KING.

Not by the Saxon chief on whom you call
In your vain arrogance, you bold, bad man;
But by the holy and the blessed saints
We swear that we would take you at your word,
Did we consider you alone in this;
And deem the land, thus purged of feverish heat,
More fit abode for men!

HAROLD.

My gracious liege,
My brother's sword hath ever fenced your throne;

Let this his service in the past plead now,
When, in the heat of passion, he hath erred.
His hasty words he will in penitence
Retract, and bow unto deserved reproof;
Before the witan will he plead his cause
In all the circumstance of Gamel's death.
Let not his angry words be filed against him.

TOSTIG.

Thanks, prudent brother; who would shape your course
With nice diplomacy through crooked ways!
What are a brother's claims or kindred ties
To him whose wisdom brothers every one?
I will not plead my cause before the witan;
I am an earl, and in my veins the blood
Of warrior kings.   The thing I did, I stand to;
It was a right pertaining to my earldom.
Let thanes in witan try the acts of thanes;
I am above their law; I laugh at them.

HAROLD.

Peace, Tostig; you are so inflamed with wrath
That anger smothers reason.   Leave with me
The vindication of this act, and I will plead
Your cause unto the king and to the witan.

TOSTIG.

My cause with you, unnatural brother! No!

Draws his sword and advances toward HAROLD,
but is held back by GUTHLAC *and the guards,*
who interpose between them and surround
TOSTIG.

If I must choose a champion for my right,
Svend, King of Denmark, or my Norman brother
Shall stand for me. How like you these, my lords?

To the KING *while sheathing his sword.*

Nay, do not fear me, sainted Majesty;
I will not break your guard.

KING.

Take him away—

A berserker! a firebrand! He is possessed.

The guards look to HAROLD *who hesitates, then*
waves his hand sadly, and TOSTIG *is led off.*

Alas, such strife is mortal to this land!
Lo! a prophetic vision comes to me:
Discord is sitting on this island throne
With frenzy in her eyes; her hands upraised
Urge on tumultuous war; the affrighted land
Trembles to hear the din. I will not see it;
It terrifies my soul. Upon my knees,
O England, I have prayed to all the saints

For your prosperity, but yet in vain;
The portents in my heart foreshadow woe l

MORKAR.

Much woe must England suffer if, O King,
Such earls as this shall rule within her realm.

ARCHBISHOP ALDRED.

My liege, Earl Godwin was my youth's best friend,
And deep the debt of gratitude I owe
Which I would pay his sons; yet larger still
The debt I owe my country.   Not in haste
I counsel should Earl Tostig's acts be judged,
But with the ripest wisdom.   In our land
Two powers build up the state: the power of God,
Its exponent the holy church,—and law,
Its exponent the king.   By law the king
Hath rights executive, as hath each earl
And every ealdorman; the meanest ceorl
Hath yet his rights, as firmly built on law
As are the king's.   Allow these laws to fail
As they pertain to ceorl, earl or king,
And all the body of our state is threatened
With overthrow.   This do I urge to show,
Though Tostig's office give prescriptive rights,
It doth not give the power to fix those rights;

Nor king nor earl can stand above the law
As angry Tostig claims.

ARCHBISHOP STIGAND.

        In state affairs,—
Indeed in all affairs, or great or small,—
Beside the right and law, another claim
Oft presses into council, which men call
Expediency.   Earl Tostig is allied
To Norman William through his countess, Judith,
And to her father, Baldwin Count of Flanders;
Then through his mother to the Danish king;
Three warlike potentates, whose enmity
Might bring more evil than we seek to cure.

KING.

Earl Morkar, we defer to render judgment
Till further counsel.   May the saints bestow
Such worldly wisdom as may cure this strife
Of angry men!
HAROLD.

      My liege, I ask your leave
To go, your envoy, into Normandy,
And bring my kindred from Duke William's court.
Your royal cousin holds unlawfully
The hostages that my dead father gave,

His pledge to you; nor heeds the messengers
Sent to recall my kinsmen from his court:
Me, he would heed; my visiting perhaps
Draw closer ties of friendship and alliance.

KING.

Nay, nay, son Harold; here you surely err,
Trusting yourself in Norman William's power.
God sends an ominous chill upon our heart
Hearing your desperate purpose — Leave the realm
While thus men's passions clamor in our court,
With broil and murder rife throughout the land,
When none but you can quell each rising storm,
No one like you support our feeble hand?
Oh, Harold, this from you! We pardon Tostig;
So you will stay with us, ask what you will:
But do not threaten to desert your king.

HAROLD.

Your Majesty hath no more faithful servant
Than Harold Godwinson will ever prove,
Who will desert you never. I but go
On a brief embassy to friendly court;
You scarce shall miss me ere I will return;
During my absence Gurth and Leofwine
Shall be to you as Harold.

KING.

                    Though I know well,
Son Harold, that your worldly wisdom looks
Beyond the sight and reach of other men,
I apprehend some peril to our land
Lurking behind this purpose, hid from you,
But darkly shadowed in my prophet-heart.
I cannot make you stay; but if you go,
O holy saints! absolve me from the sin,
And spare my eyes the misery to see
The monstrous ills, whose huge impending shade
Falls darkly at my feet.   (*Rises.*) Your arm, my son,
To help our feeble steps.

          The KING *leans on* HAROLD, *descends from his*
               throne, and passes out with guards, attendants,
               etc. ARCHBISHOP STIGAND *detains* ALDRED.

ARCHBISHOP STIGAND.

                    Aldred, the king
Grows feebler every day, and, like a child,
Sees shadows in the dark: he needs the help
Of some firm mind to regulate his own;
To shape and give direction to his acts.
In Harold's absence we may mould the king,
And higher build our holy church of God.

ARCHBISHOP ALDRED.

Aye, for the present; but I look beyond,
And see upon the throne another king,
Who may not be so friendly to our church
As pious Edward, soon to be a saint.

Exeunt.

SCENE III.—LONDON.

*A chamber in the Benedictine Abbey.   A table with
papers, pen and ink.*

ARCHBISHOP ALDRED *seated and* EARL MORKAR *standing.*

MORKAR.

In vain you counsel patience while I see
These hungry Godwinsons devour the land.
Who hold the three great earldoms? Sons of Godwin.
Northumbria's Tostig's, and rich Mercia, Gurth's;
The while my father's sons, the heirs of Mercia,
And Waltheof, heir of all Northumbria,
Must be contented with estates of thanes.
South of the Thames spreads Harold's earldom broad;
Nor this alone, although an earl in name,
Harold in fact is king.   Did you not mark—
But well I know you did—how our sick king

Speaks but the words that Harold bids him speak?
Sees everything through Harold's thoughtful eyes?
Reflects Earl Harold as a polished mirror
Throws back a second self?   This can I bear;
For Harold, though his powerful hand has grasped
The richness and the glory of the land,
Is ever just, and looks beyond himself
To England's good.   But Tostig is all greed.
This demon son of Godwin, tiger-like,
Feeds upon England.   'Tis a wicked fiend,
That laughs alike at pity, danger, power;
Mighty of valor as the Danish Odin,
As Balder beautiful, but dread as Lok!
I, the hereditary prince of Mercia,
Am set aside, while this fierce pirate rules;
Nor only rules, the earl of broad domains,
But sends his spoilers over all the land.
O father, preach not your dull virtue, patience,
To one who feels his native rights abused;
To one who sees his friends and kinsmen slain,
His country's laws and customs set at naught
By a wild viking, whose bold, scornful laugh
Derides the king, defies the hand of power!

ARCHBISHOP ALDRED.

Didst mark his shrewd intent when the Archbishop

Of Canterbury gave counsel to the king,
How he advised this thing, expediency,
To sit above our judgments?   It is true:
What is our right we often must defer
Because such right is barred from us by that
Would cost us much to push aside; so you,
Who cannot reach at once what is your right,
Must bear your wrong because expediency
Stays present having.

MORKAR.

        Patience supposes hope;
But what have I on which to build a hope?
While I must wait the wrong grows daily more;
And I shall wake to hear fierce Tostig's band
Batter upon my gate; and then my waiting,
Like Gamel's, stop.

ARCHBISHOP ALDRED.

        Pray tell me this, my son:
Whose is the greatest name and power in England?

MORKAR.

Harold's.

ARCHBISHOP ALDRED.

And who will sit on England's throne

When sainted Edward puts aside its crown
To wear the one, won by his holy life?

MORKAR.

I cannot tell—The power of force so rules,
How can I know Tostig will not be king?

ARCHBISHOP ALDRED.

Harold will be the king.

MORKAR.

What hope for me,
For England, when fierce Tostig shall have scope
For all his lawlessness, thus near the throne?

ARCHBISHOP ALDRED.

Wisdom should teach you how to gain allies
Whose help may safely fence you from attack
Of him you fear.

MORKAR.

You surely mock me, father;
Allies against the powerful Godwinsons!
No man can stand against them in this land.

ARCHBISHOP ALDRED.

I did not say against the Godwinsons;
But Tostig only.

MORKAR.

That is still the same ;
Will Harold cleave to me, forsake his brother ?

ARCHBISHOP ALDRED.

Yes, if you are his brother.

MORKAR.

Show your riddle ;
I have no heart or patience to be guessing ;
Tell me in plainness what your meaning is.

ARCHBISHOP ALDRED.

My son, in plainness, I would bid you wed
Your sister, Aldyth, to fierce Tostig's brother.

MORKAR.

To Harold ?   Nay ; his heart is fast enchained
By the fair Swan-neck, lovely Lady Edith ;
Such chains as hers are hard to break apart.
Father, you counsel things impossible.

ARCHBISHOP ALDRED.

I think not so.   In Harold's royal heart,
Above all other impulse and intent,

D   7

Is zeal for England; by this grander love
He may be brought to yield his passionate hopes,
Though in the act his generous heart be torn.
Give your consent, and frame your sister to it;
My part shall be—indeed a cruel one—
To make the Earl resign his cherished love,
Although she be our England's fairest flower,
And wed your sister.   This I undertake
Not all to help you, but to help our land,
That needs, I fear, in troublous times to come,
The strongest bonds of unity between
Our diverse peoples, a true brotherhood
Of Godwin's heirs and those of Leofric.

MORKAR.

Father, I give consent; and I will prove,
If Harold wed my sister, true to him;
So shall he sit secure on England's throne.
Although a son of Godwin rules in Mercia,
The heirs of Leofric rule Mercia's hearts:
Thus I can bring to Harold stronger help
Than seems proportioned to my present power.

ARCHBISHOP ALDRED.

'Tis well, and therefore I have counseled patience;
Avoid all contest with Northumbria's Earl,

For he may crush you if you drive him to it;
But in the future Mercia may be yours,
Yours the broad earldom Leofric once held,
If with due caution the safe track you steer,
Learning the lesson: Fortune's oftener won
By wise diplomacy than brutal strength.

MORKAR.

Father, I yield me to your larger wisdom,
Keeping alight the hopes that you have kindled,
And wait with patience for a better time;
Meanwhile I'll do your bidding: so farewell!

> *Kneels and receives the blessing of* ARCHBISHOP
> ALDRED, *then exit.*

ARCHBISHOP ALDRED.

The Welsh king's widow, Aldyth, wed to Harold,
Will bring her husband a rich wedding dower,
The hearts of Mercia.   Wessex is his,
And Kent; all Saxon England clings to him
Because his heart is Saxon.   He will have
Northumbria's love in right of Danish blood
Transmitted through his noble mother, Gytha,
From Woden's stock; so will his kingdom stand.

> ARCHBISHOP ALDRED *sits.*

Oh for the power of mind that looks beyond

This creeping present into future years,
Sees in the acts of men, their forms of thought,
Speech, fashions, tendencies, beliefs, desires,
The living letters that make up the words
In which is writ the coming of the future,
Of men and states, the fateful destinies !
Around me jar confusing elements,
Which I would so direct that holy church,
Our Saxon church of England, may increase
In power to mould the hearts and acts of men
To greater glory of the living God
And us, his faithful servants in the church.
But yet I see not clear ; I fear each act
May, like a weapon in unskillful hand,
Effect not benefit, but injury.
The papal sceptre stretches out from Rome
Over the churches with an iron rule ;
The tiara changes to a golden crown,
And crosiers into swords.   Alas the day !
Our Saxon fashions are deemed out of date
By those of Rome ; while the great cardinal,
Ambitious Hildebrand, behind the pope,
Waits but the moment of auspicious time
To modernize our simple, Saxon church
By gathering in one grasp its several powers ;
Even as Guiscard or aspiring William

Would overthrow our Saxon liberties,
Could either gain a foothold in the land.
Walks up and down impatiently.
Oh for a larger intellectual grasp,
That I may utilize each circumstance,
And mould the men and times into safe means
To keep unaltered customs as of old,
Our ancient privilege, prescriptive rights !
But while I strive to shape a wholesome scheme
The thought forever haunts me that my plans
May but precipitate catastrophe ;
Yet I must build them, or to stand or fall,
As Providence, more wise than I, ordains.
I fear the Norman most, and think 'tis plain
The safest way to hold this danger off
Is to consolidate the power of Harold,
That when he sits upon the English throne,
And holds his sceptre o'er our Saxon church,
That sceptre may have power still to preclude
The innovations of intriguing Rome
Which Norman rule would quickly fasten here ;
So I have set my plans.
He sits again.
It is full time
The Lady Edith came upon my summons ;
I have determined so to place this thing

Before her generous mind that her own act
May break the chains enthralling Harold's heart;
Thus may I model his less plastic mind
To equal sacrifice.

Enter an attendant.

ATTENDANT.

The Lady Edith.

ARCHBISHOP ALDRED.

Bring her to me.

Exit attendant.

Now must I steel myself
Against all soft emotion, nor consent
To feel the thrills of human tenderness.

Enter attendant ushering the LADY EDITH; *exit
attendant.*

EDITH.

My holy father.

Edith kneels to ARCHBISHOP ALDRED, *and receives
his blessing.*

ARCHBISHOP ALDRED.

Bless you, my fair child,
Who come thus dutifully to my call;

The young and beautiful, in full pursuit
Of pleasures and the joys of opening life,
Not always listen to a sober voice
Calling their thoughts to higher, nobler things
Than butterfly-existence.　I am glad
My daughter is not so in pleasures steeped
As to neglect my call.

EDITH.

Most holy sir,
Think not that pleasure only rules my heart;
For though, like all possessing youth and health,
I feel the charms of beauty and sweet hope
Thrill my young blood, make my quick pulses beat,
And life rejoice in brightness, yet indeed
I have my graver hours; and then I know
That life is not alone for idle pleasure,
But for the larger hopes and destinies
Of us, who play awhile among the flowers,
But must at last take each the several tasks
And graver duties of a serious world.

ARCHBISHOP ALDRED.

I am much pleased, dear daughter, that your mind
Reasons thus wisely in the midst of pleasures;
For now I know, when duty points the way,

Your heart will yield desirings, wrong though sweet,
And that your steps will press the better path.

EDITH.

What is it, father, that you ask of me?
Have I then seemed too fond of worldly pleasures,
Nor given unto God and holy church
Fit portion of my time? If this be so,
I take your chiding in much penitence,
And, humbly craving pardon, still will strive
To sin less in the future; for in truth
I have such serious yearnings and intents
That I can fondly give my time to holy thoughts.

ARCHBISHOP ALDRED.

I cannot blame you, daughter, for the past;
Your life hath ever been a blameless one;
But now the hour is come for sober thought:
Your country and our holy church require
Your best assistance in a time of need.

EDITH.

My father, I? And can I help my country?
                Aside.
O Harold, this will bring me nearer you!

ARCHBISHOP ALDRED.

Even you, fair daughter ; your white hands are weak ;
You cannot toil, nor fight, yet you can give
Something to help your country. Think, my child :
Can you consent to yield your dearest wish
That thus your country may be made more happy ?

EDITH.

My dearest wish ! Father, what do you ask ?
My heart so flutters that I cannot think—
You know not what may be my dearest wish.

ARCHBISHOP ALDRED.

Yes, child, I know it ; and it grieves me much
There to disturb your heart's tranquillity ;
But long ago I taught myself to yield
Dear yearnings for the greater good of all,
And know each generous act repays itself.
That fondest, brightest hope of your young life
Is the one sacrifice your country asks.

EDITH.

To give up Harold ? Oh, my father, say
I have mistaken what you ask of me !
Do not ask that : my heart to kill my heart,
Killing the hope in which alone I live.

D*   F

ARCHBISHOP ALDRED.

Dear child, when duty sadly points the way
To sacrifice, the heart in agony
Thinks life a desert, robbed of one bright hope,
And duty odious, though the call of God.

EDITH, *kneeling.*

Father, upon my knees I pray of you
Leave me this hope, so twined around my life
That when its tendrils shall be torn away
My pulse can never beat again one healthful throb,
And I will give you all the rest beside :
Ask what you will ; my fortune and my time
I will devote ; my hands and brain shall toil,
Oh, always faithfully, to do your work !
But spare my heart ! oh, father, spare my heart !

ARCHBISHOP ALDRED.

Your hands and brain can give no useful help
Unto your country.　By this sacrifice
Of fond affection only can you prove
Yourself above the selfishness that clings
To some desired thing, though all the world
Suffer while you indulge your selfish longings.

EDITH, *rising, and haughtily.*

Why do I kneel to you? What right have you
To bid me crush my heart and its best hopes,
That some vain plan, born of your scheming brain,
May thus be helped? This faithful love of mine
By God implanted, nourished in my breast,
Is not for priests to censure; God alone,
Who gave it, hath the right to take it from me.

ARCHBISHOP ALDRED.

God filled your breast with love, that thus his child
Might have a worthy gift of sacrifice
To lay before his feet. Think not, vain one,
That you alone of all God's children here
Are called upon to yield to him your hopes:
Thousands on thousands struggled in the past,
Thousands to-day fight their rebellious hearts
As you must, child. Pray God to guide you right.

EDITH.

Why do you choose me from a thousand others
To bid me thus, in life's most pleasant bloom,
Give up the brightness of the cheerful day,
Enrobe myself in darkness of the tomb?
Hope's radiance quenched, there is no other light;

Life without Harold is a dismal night.
Why should my body live, and my heart dead?
Oh, father, it was only yesterday
He told me that he loved me; and to-day
You ask me to give up his glorious love,
Mine only for one day!   Alas! I cannot.
You ask too much of a poor, trembling child
Who hath not courage for this suicide.

ARCHBISHOP ALDRED.

Listen, my daughter: in the name of duty
I have required this heavy sacrifice,
That thus, by yielding, you may win the glory,
The martyr's glory of beneficence:
Now will I add to holy duty, reason,
To help you quell the longings of your heart.
Earl Harold will be king; at Edward's death
The witan will confer a crown on him:
But will he rule?   No easy seat for him,
This island throne.   The Dane; the Norman Duke;
Friends of the Ætheling; Morkar and Edwin,
Grandsons of Leofric; young Waltheof,
Great Siward's heir; Hakon and Tostig fierce,
His nephew and his brother;—all may claim
And struggle for his throne.   No hope for him,
For England's peace, for God's most holy church

In England, if the new king do not hold
The hearts of all his people.   Ancient names
Live through the change of rule, and hold the hearts
Hereditary of a glory-loving race
Fast in the chains of legend and of song;
Earl Harold hath no hold on Mercia:
As king, he cannot hope to have its help
Unless he make alliance with its lords,
The heirs of Leofric.   By wedding Aldyth
He gains all Mercia, as her wedding gift.

EDITH.

Harold wed Aldyth?—O my heart, be still!

ARCHBISHOP ALDRED.

Grand is the front of kingly majesty,
Godlike its power; but yet the monarch pays
A cruel price to sit beside the gods—
As we poor priests pay for the kingly right
To be God's ministers upon the earth.
Out of his heart, his pitiless hand must tear
Each hope whose budding whispers happiness:
He lives for all, not for his single self;
The love of chosen mate is not for him;
His country claims his hand to marry states,
Making alliance by his marriage rites.

8

So Power, in dreary isolation, stands;
And Greatness towers above life's broken hopes.

EDITH.

But will Earl Harold so consent to yield
Himself in purchase of this barren power?

ARCHBISHOP ALDRED.

He must consent, if in his generous soul
The love of England lingers as of old.
Not for the pride and crown of majesty,
Nor even for the fame and large renown
Of kingly acts, may Harold give up love;
But when his country, helpless and alarmed,
Calls on the patriot for his sacrifice,
Then would you have your Harold answer, "No;"
Regardful only of his selfish love?
Or would you have his noble heart respond
Though all its tendrils bled in sundering love?

EDITH.

Nay, do not ask me, father—in my brain
All is confusion; and my heart is stone.

ARCHBISHOP ALDRED.

Think well of this, my child: at duty's call

Harold must cancel promised love to you,
Or, placing you beside him on the throne,
Feel his throne totter, and at last o'erturned,
Fall in the general ruin of the state ;
While England echoes everywhere the cry,
"The king hath brought this ruin on his land
Because he would not yield his fond desire
For a fair, selfish woman."
Then you may see in his sad eyes reproach ;
In place of love, dread hauntings of remorse.
'Tis yours, my child, to make a nobler choice—
Do you give up the Earl, thus sparing him
That painful, passionate struggle of the breast
When Duty is compelled to drive out Love—
Thus will you earn the glorious recompense
Of generous act, a sweet approving voice
Telling of nobler life than Love's vain dream,
Whose beauty fadeth while its joys are grasped ;
Thus will you show your king how a pure soul
Hath worth of virtue, strength of purity
To choose aright the better path of life,
Renouncing Love at Duty's holy call.

EDITH.

Father, no more—no more !—My heart is breaking !
Leave me ; and when my agony is less,

And thought controls again my dizzy brain,
I'll give an answer—if I live to give it.

ARCHBISHOP ALDRED.

Pardon me, daughter, for this cruel pain ;
But Duty is the cause, and I, her servant
Who grieve, but must perform a cruel part.

> ARCHBISHOP ALDRED *extends his hands over the
> head of* EDITH, *who has fallen on her knees.*

Bless her, O Saints, and give her healing strength !

> *Exit* ARCHBISHOP ALDRED.

EDITH.

Alas ! alas !—my broken, broken heart !
> EDITH *falls prostrate on the floor.*

ACT III.

SCENE I.—LONDON.

The house of Countess Gytha. Gytha *seated and*
Tostig *standing.*

Gytha.

You too will leave me!   Ah, how desolate
Grows day by day my hearthstone !   Wolnoth first ;
Then my brave Sweyn ; your noble father next ;
Then Harold ; now, my Tostig, you must go.
Like blasted trunk of a storm-broken oak,
I shall be left, all my proud branches gone.

Tostig.

They drive me from you, mother, from my land,
And set their outlawry upon my head—
This witan of the ealdormen and priests—
And Morkar is to have Northumbria,
My earldom—Fools !—They should cut off my head ;
And so they would, but dare not—Hunt the lion
To drive him from his jungle, but not dare

To bring the brute to bay !   Let them beware
The hour he comes to hunt the huntsmen ; then
Will his roaring terrify their timid hearts !—
Mother, I thank you for my Danish blood ;
Now, viking-like, I have no lands, no home ;
Over the swan's-bath shall my long-ships drive ;
A king of Ocean will the wolf's-head be—
A wolf's-head !—Who will take it ?—Mother, mark :
I will return with warriors of the North ;
Our bright round shields will glisten in the sun,
A shining row along each dragon's side ;
Our war-songs loudly ring along these shores,
And fright their witans—Mother, I must go.

GYTHA.

My son, will you then war upon your land ?

TOSTIG.

Mother, I have no land: they banish me.

GYTHA.

You are too wild, my son ; remember Sweyn ;
His wayward passions wrecked my eldest son :
Curb your fierce wrath, and take the wise advice
Of Harold, who will give you back again

Your former honors ; shape your life like his,
And stand among the foremost of the land.

TOSTIG.

No, mother ; in my veins the viking-blood
Runs all too hot to be another Harold
And smile where I would strike.

*Walks away impatiently, then returns and kneels
to* GYTHA.

I kiss your hands,
My mother, and I bow to you my head.
Your Harold will return from Normandy
To care for you ; he hath a prudent brain,
He will not be a wolf's-head : but for me,
I cannot stay.
Yet you shall hear of Tostig.   When the winds
Blow their wild blasts out of the stormy north,
Then listen, mother, for my battle-songs ;
They shall be heard anon.   Mother, farewell.
In Tostig's heart, though fierce and wild it be,
There's yet a tender part that throbs for thee.

GYTHA, *embracing* TOSTIG.

My son.   Thou hast a sea-king's stormy soul—
True offspring of the Dane.   Whate'er your fate,

And much my soul forebodes unhappy chance,
Your mother's love will cling to you till death.

Exit TOSTIG.

May all the saints protect my outlawed son,
My warrior son, so beautiful and brave;
More like the fabled gods of the old North,
Than the tame men of this degenerate day!

Enter GURTH, *and after him* GUTHLAC.

GURTH.

My mother.

GYTHA.

Gurth, what news of Harold?

She sees GUTHLAC.

Speak,

Thane Guthlac—if but brief my greeting seem,
Think that a mother asks you for her sons,
Waiting for news through all these weary months.

GUTHLAC.

Most noble lady, the Earl, your son, is come;
And I am sent before to give you news.

GYTHA.

Doth he bring Wolnoth? and Sweyn's boy, young
Hakon?

GURTH.

Nay, mother; Harold's peril hath been great :
To do your bidding, and bring back your son,
My brother risked the glory of our house.

GUTHLAC.

Lady, your grandson, Hakon, comes with Harold,
But Wolnoth tarries in Duke William's court;
There he hath health and friends and pleasant cheer,
Nor brighter shines on Leofwine's fair brow
The laughing smile, than smiles your Wolnoth's face.
He sends his duty and his love to you.

GYTHA.

Once more must hope in disappointment sink—
But what the peril Harold hath endured?

GUTHLAC.

First shipwreck on the coast of Ponthieu;
Escaped the sea, a prisoner to Count Guy;
From thence transferred by ransom to Duke William.
This placed him in the crafty Norman's power
Without restraints of hospitality,
On which, and courtesy, he counted much
When first he purposed visiting the Duke.

GYTHA.

Did not Duke William treat him as a guest,
An honored guest, the equal of himself?

GUTHLAC.

Craft is the Norman's weapon : like a brother
Duke William took him in his arms, and placed him
Beside himself, upon an equal seat ;
Gave sumptuous banquets, more magnificent
And costly than our English monarchs have ;
Amused us with rich shows, gay pageants, tilts,
Keeping our Earl always beside himself ;
Made war on Conan, Duke of Brittany,
To show the martial training of his knights :
In which, a short campaign, like loving brothers,
Earl Harold and Duke William fought together,
Shared the same tent and table, and at night
Stretched side by side, in slumber, on one bed.
When in the field, Earl Harold shone a king
Among their Norman knights—his martial deeds
The theme of every tongue ; but when at last
He asked the hostages, to make an end
Of pleasant visiting, the subtle Norman
Claimed England as a promise from our king,
His kinsman ; and required his guest's sworn oath

To be his man : exacting this great price
For hospitality—

GURTH.

'Twas Circe's price,
Manhood for blandishments.

GYTHA.

My son, his man !
How answered Harold ?

GUTHLAC.

So the snare was spread
The Earl was meshed, whichever way he turned :
If he refused, a prison waited him,
And England was made helpless, lacking him
To bar the Norman ; if he should consent,
His oath would fortify the claim alleged
Of Edward's former promise to his cousin.

GURTH.

To meet such craft, there was no way but craft—
The lion learns a lesson of the fox.

GUTHLAC.

And so I deem Earl Harold answered it :
He gave consent to all the Duke's demands ;
Betrothed himself to the young Adeliza ;

Before an assembly of the Norman states
Took oath of service upon cross and relic
To William's future crown.   Again was craft—
A cunning trap prepared to catch his soul
If he should dare deny these oaths compelled :
While the Earl's hand was laid upon the cross,
And on his lip the vow, a juggling priest
Drew off the altar-covering, and displayed,
Beneath, a heap of relics,—bones of saints
Gathered from all the shrines throughout the land,—
A dismal charnel-house where superstition
Grinned on the luckless swearer.   Pale as death
Which thus mocked at him, our brave Harold stood ;
But not a tremor shook his steady tones
Repeating oaths to these grim witnesses.
This mock of sacred ceremony done,
Again Earl Harold claimed the hostages
And leave to go.
Again the crafty Norman showed his guile :
He gave up Hakon, but kept Wolnoth back,
His hostage for Earl Harold's faith to him.
As thus we left perfidious Normandy,
Upon Earl Harold's face a look of gloom
Hung heavy, on his cloudy brow a frown ;
Scarcely a word he spake until once more
His foot was set upon the soil of Sussex,

When, lifting up his head, he cried aloud,
"Absolve me, saints, whose bones have been profaned
By jugglers' tricks, and mocked by perfidy!"

GYTHA.

Alas! what dark misfortune hides in this?
I feel its boding shadow cross my heart
That coldly shudders with an ague-thrill.

GURTH.

It was a mean and treacherous deceit,
A trick, whose cunning cheats the crafty knave,
Duke though he be, that planned its tangled snare;
For such offense to honesty absolves
The swearer from the duty of his oaths.
Mother, farewell—I go to Harold.

GUTHLAC.
                                        Pardon

Me, noble lady, that I bring ill news
Which I wished better.

GYTHA.

                    Thanks for your better wish.
                        Exeunt GURTH *and* GUTHLAC.
O Wolnoth! shall I never see thee more?   *Exit.*

SCENE II.—LONDON.

A chamber in the Benedictine Abbey. A table covered with papers, at which is seated ARCHBISHOP ALDRED.

ARCHBISHOP ALDRED.

Thus, like magician Merlin in his cell,
I shape the fortunes of the coming time.
That dream of eld, the force of magic art
Was but the might of intellectual thought
Stamped on the ignorance of a rude age.
Over the seas from Rome's imperial site
I feel the force of Hildebrand's large brain;
But thus I counterplot to build a throne
Between our Saxon church and Italy;
And all goes well.   Morkar will give his sister,
The ealdormen their votes, to Saxon Harold;
And Saxon Harold will protect the church.
Tostig is banished; thus an element
Of discord is removed.   Harold returned
And wed to Aldyth, all my plans are safe;
And Hildebrand's ambitious strivings, checked,
Will find a limit in the narrow seas

That roll between our isle and Normandy.
Yes, this is my enchantment—

        Enter HAROLD *hurriedly.*

                Who art thou
That come so roughly on my presence?—Harold!

HAROLD.

O holy father, help my troubled soul,
Fighting a cruel battle in this breast!

ARCHBISHOP ALDRED.

Shield us, O saints!   Son Harold, what is this?

HAROLD.

This is it: I have sworn a wicked oath:
Which is the greater sin, to keep such oath:
Or break it?

        ARCHBISHOP ALDRED.

        Tell me first, my son, what oath
You have so rashly sworn.

HAROLD.

        Fool that I was
To venture in the Norman spider's power!

ARCHBISHOP ALDRED.

Yield not to passion's storm; but speak more calmly.

HAROLD.

Calmly!

ARCHBISHOP ALDRED.

Yes; calmly.

HAROLD.

     If my whirling brain
Will let me, father, I will tell you all.
In my mind's vanity I reasoned thus:
I know the measure of Duke William's mind;
He is ambitious, but delights in honor
And all the noble usage of that code
Of knighthood that he fosters in his land.
O father, I was blind—as Folly, blind;
I did not know the man. His knighthood's code
Is but a cloak he wears to hide his heart,
Swollen to bursting with ambition, greed.
Religion, knighthood, cunning, are the tools
His will and huge ambition wield to build
Aloft his fortunes. Father, I fear the man;
His wicked genius will o'erride my force:
But, by my soul's eternal life, I swear

That I will fight his fortunes, step by step,
Ere he shall build his throne in my dear land!

ARCHBISHOP ALDRED.

Nay, speak more calmly, Harold; tell me all.

HAROLD.

I thought that I was safe, trusting his honor;
And this hath wrecked me.   Once within his power
I was as helpless as a fly immeshed
By cunning spider.   In his smile I saw,
Long ere his words told me his heart's desire,
How I had lost my venture in his land.
Day after day. I watched his crafty face,
And, underneath vain compliments, beheld
How eagerly he sought to read my mind,
That his might rightly weave his subtle plans.
Then came a deep resolve upon my soul
To meet his craft with like, and baffle him
With the same art by which he sought his ends.
This is the sin hath blackened all my life.
O father, weary, weary were the days
We watched each other, and I masked my thought
Under a constant smile; but he, more bold,
Because he held the chances in his hand,
Hid not his purpose from me, though not yet

Shaped in his words; and still the problem worked,
Whether to crush, or use me.   When at length
Determined in his course, he questioned me
If I would help him to the throne of England
When vacant by the death of our King Edward,
Whose heir he was by Edward's solemn promise.
What could I answer, father, to his question?

ARCHBISHOP ALDRED.

A negative had cost you then your life?

HAROLD.

As surely as this Norman's vast ambition
Will cost our land a hecatomb of lives:
Which to avert, my own most cheerfully
I would have yielded him; but dying thus,
Who would be left to warn, or happily save
My country?

ARCHBISHOP ALDRED.

A promise thus extorted
In peril of your life is null and void.

HAROLD.

But listen, father.   In the solemn presence
Of the assembled states my oath was made

Upon a cross and relic; while I swore,
Odo of Bayeux, with sardonic grin,
Drew off the cloth of gold beneath my hand,
And, lo! a coffer filled with dead men's bones
Was there; and I had filed the prescribed oaths
Upon the relics of a hundred saints
Gathered from all the shrines in Normandy.

ARCHBISHOP ALDRED, *aside.*

I see the hand of Hildebrand in this.

HAROLD.

It was a juggler's trick—fit for a fiend,
Not for a Christian priest.   Then William's eye
As glittering as a basilisk's was fixed
On me, and its grim triumph haunts me now.

ARCHBISHOP ALDRED.

Truly, my son, your oaths were greatly sealed :
And though you knew not of the coffered bones,
Yet do they bind your soul.   But be of cheer ;
The church of Christ, thus symbolized by saints,
Can set you free from these entangling oaths ;
Which profit not the church, nor holy saints,
Profit no good, but help an evil thing.

HAROLD.

Until the hour the Norman Duke entrapped me
I kept my soul, in honest purpose, clear;
But now 'tis stained and darkened by a crime:
Nor, though the church absolve me of each oath,
Can I win back the pure white garb of Truth.

ARCHBISHOP ALDRED.

Nay, Harold, if the church absolve the oath
Your soul is clear; all stains thus washed away.

HAROLD.

Father, before this sin, with hope and faith
In my true purpose and my honest heart,
I faced the future: now as black as night
Seem all forebodingly the days to come;
Nor lighted by one cheerful ray of hope.

ARCHBISHOP ALDRED.

Thus is it ever, my dear son, with error;
It blackens all things, but it makes most foul
The spot where it abides. If you have erred
It was through erring judgment, and the sin
Hath no abiding-place within your soul.
Are you content your penance for this error

Shall be the true devotion of yourself
Unto your country?

HAROLD.

If, thus sin-begrimed,
I can be deemed still worthy to do this,
My single aim shall be to save my land
From the insatiate lust of the fierce tiger
That I have seen stretching his huge, sharp claws
Out of their velvet sheaths, in hungry greed
To feed on England.

ARCHBISHOP ALDRED.

England and freedom rest on you alone—
Our free-born England and our Saxon freedom.
There is no other chief in all the land
Can cope with William, or can lead, as thou,
United England forth—a mighty host
Whose myriad swords will cut to finest shreds
The cunning plans of these intriguing foes.
Yet think not, Harold, this great duty easy;
Who gives himself, must not hold back a part:
Your country needs your greatest sacrifice.

HAROLD.

What mean you, father?   What more can I give
Than the true service of my mind and hands?

E*

ARCHBISHOP ALDRED.

You must give up another plighted promise—
Not, like these last, sworn to unwillingly.

HAROLD.

Another promise! you must mean, to Edith.
How can my love for her obstruct my service
And duty to my country?

ARCHBISHOP ALDRED.

Thus, my son:
To bind the country to you, heart and hand,
The heirs of Godwin and of Leofric
Must make alliance with a stronger bond
Than the large promises that men forget.
This bond must be your marriage with fair Aldyth.

HAROLD.

No, priest; I give my country earnest work,
Untiring labor of my mind and hands;
My heart is plighted to the Lady Edith,
And it were mockery of faith and truth
To wed another.

ARCHBISHOP ALDRED.

Is it even so?

England hath only one great Saxon left,
Inheritor of her brave people's love,
With strength of mind and arm to help her now,
And he would rather wanton in the smile
Of a fair woman, than protect his land
From a dread foe, armed with the potent might
And subtle pretext of these broken oaths?
For, as your dark forebodings indicate,
Your mind perceives how this unhappy chance
May prove a weapon in the Norman's hand
To strike your country its most deadly blow.

HAROLD.

Father, I see it; and it is this thought
That drives my mind to chaos of despair.
Since my rash oath, thus sealed by trickery
With the tremendous seal of superstition,
I see its several imports, hidden then
When on my startled mind the trap was sprung.
Thus hampered I am all unfit to be the king;
Let England choose another; I will serve him.

ARCHBISHOP ALDRED.

You speak not now like Harold. Look around;
Where is the king to place on England's throne?

HAROLD.

Edgar the Ætheling.

ARCHBISHOP ALDRED.

   Nay, Harold; shame
Should seal your lips from speaking such poor folly;
Edmund's weak grandson cannot be our king.

HAROLD.

My arm will guard his sceptre, prop his throne.

ARCHBISHOP ALDRED.

Peace!—Edgar matched against the Norman Duke—
The folly of the thing would stir men's laughter,
Did not its peril strike their lips with palsy.

HAROLD.

O priest, you hotly chase my panting heart,
As hunters chase the timid, flying deer
From covert unto covert, till at last,
Beat from all refuge, there is naught but death.

ARCHBISHOP ALDRED.

I only show you what yourself will see,
Without such showing, when the time matures,
That thus forewarned you may be well prepared.

HAROLD.

No, no; my arm would lose both skill and strength;
Courage forsake me, yielding cherished hope;
And judgment too desert my unnerved brain,
If I should forfeit truth and manhood thus.

ARCHBISHOP ALDRED.

Howe'er you strive against the inevitable,
God, duty, and your conscience still remain,
And point the path your foot must surelv tread.

HAROLD.

I come to you for comfort, and you give
Me up to torture.

ARCHBISHOP ALDRED.

    Midst a thousand pangs
That tear the body and distract the soul,
That soul springs upward to a better life
From painful bed of death; so life's large aims
Are won by suffering and the wreck of hopes:
You only bear, my son, your share of pain;
Many there be who bear a double load.

HAROLD.

God guide me rightly, for my stubborn heart

Rebels against the duty that you teach !
Pray for me, father ; and discharge the oaths
Whose burden on my conscience weighs me down
So heavily that duty strikes my ear,
A senseless word, with scarce a meaning to it.

Exeunt.

SCENE III.—LONDON.

The house of EDITH.

Enter EDITH, *dressed in black, and with a sad countenance.*

EDITH.

How strange it seems the sun should shine so bright,
The birds so gayly sing upon the boughs
Of the old Druid oak beside my lattice,
And in the garden where I loved to walk
The flowers should open blossoms to the sun,
And insects flit—huge, bright-winged butterflies,
Swift bees, gold-ringed, darting with busy hum—
All summer-like, and gay with glad rejoicing,
While in my bosom freezing winter reigns,

And happiness—a vanished dream—appears
Only a recollection of the past!
Alas! insensible the busy world
Of nature, heedless all, while sorrow feeds,
Like a devouring moth, within my breast.
It seems as if the sky should take dull tints,
The sun withdraw behind black, stormy clouds,
A sudden winter freeze these summer smiles,
As youth's fond hopes are chilled and cold in me.
I thought that I must part from all these scenes
Of former happiness with sad regrets;
But now they seem so senseless of my pain,
So joyful while I weep, that thus, alas!
Even regret is lost in the cold chill
That numbs me, as I deem the hand of Death
Numbs the poor wretch it summons to the grave.
Perhaps my harp hath power to warm again
My deadened senses, as it oft hath moved,
By its sweet melodies, responsive chords
Of inner being whose vibrations stir
The quick emotions.

> *She bends over the harp, but the string she touches*
>   *breaks.*

No; its strings refuse
To yield me music, as all nature shrinks
Unsympathetic from me and my woe

Which I must bear alone.   Nothing can rouse
My stone-cold heart.

Enter a servant.

SERVANT.

My lady, the Earl Harold.

EDITH.

No—no; I cannot see him—bid him go.

Exit servant.

Why did I linger here?   My heart will break !
The abbey walls, my refuge from the world,
Should now have been my shield—

Enter HAROLD, *who advances eagerly.*

HAROLD.

My Edith—Edith—

EDITH, *shrinking back.*

Harold, I did not think to see you more ;
I have renounced the world, its joys and hopes,
For the calm stillness of a convent's cell
And blessed peace that clothes a bride of Heaven.

HAROLD.

Where is the love you promised me ?

EDITH, *laying her hand on her breast.*

Alas !

Here, Harold—here.   I cannot crush it out ;
Its roots have struck too deep.   Naught now remains
But I must hide myself and it from all
In the lone cloister.   You, to Aldyth wed,
By her alliance will protect the land ;
Edith will kiss the Saviour's holy cross.

HAROLD.

This is the work of Aldred.   Plotting priest,
Here, in the one most vulnerable spot
Of all, your keen and fatal arrow strikes !
O Edith, I have made your cherished love
My beacon-light, the bright and guiding star
To which I turn however Fortune frowns,
And in its radiance feel my strength renewed
To meet perplexities, misfortunes, doubts.
That star above me, I can smile at fate ;
With calm serenity meet any chance :
But take its light away and I am lost ;
Edith, I charge you, rob me not of hope !

' EDITH.

What should we do with hope ? that human joy

H   10*

Is not for us; cold Duty struck its blossom,
And it has withered at the icy touch.
Peasants may love and hope, but we may not.

HAROLD.

And can you, Edith, for a priest's cold words,
Give up the love you promised should be mine—
Your love, the one, sweet blossom of my hopes,
Bright childhood's promise, the very crown of life?

EDITH.

I give up you: I give not up my love;
For, Harold, I am sure, whate'er may chance,
My love and I will die in the same day.

HAROLD.

This Duty, cruel, fatal to our happiness,
Is but a phantom, summoned by a priest
To push along his nice-constructed schemes;
Our hearts and hopes, the pawns with which he plays,
Content to lose them, so he gain his end.
I too can plan as wisely as the priest;
Give me your love, and trust my larger grasp
Of statecraft and philosophy of life
That takes sufficient scope to draw within
Its figures man's humanity, as well

His generous impulse, as each cautious fear.
Thus may we serve the needs of our dear land,
And keep our hopes.   To sunder the dear ties
That we have pledged, and to go coldly out
Into the world to falsify my heart,
Would rob my arm of vigor, and my mind
Of the bright hopes, the sanguine energies,
That win success from dark, uncertain chance.
In the great game of life, 'tis not the calm,
Passionless plotter, with his deep-laid schemes,
That wins; but he within whose loving heart
Flushes the warm blood stirred by ardent hope,
The quick enthusiast, not the subtle priest.

EDITH.

O Harold, Harold, do not tempt me thus;
You know not how in anguish I have fought
My stubborn heart.   The bishop's plans are wise,
And Duty points the right but painful way;
Better to bow to Duty than Remorse.
If I should yield to you my dower might be
Sorrow, regrets, reproachful tongues of men,
Till all would look on me—yes, even you,
In spite of generous love—as the sad cause
Of your disaster and our country's ills.
Better now sorrow than a shameful end

To the proud honors, your ancestral right.
Harold, because I love you I refuse
To be the weight to pull you down from glory
And honor's bright career; so large your soul
You would give all for me : I will not take it,
And rob my country of its only help ;
Oh, let me sacrifice my heart and hopes,
Not ruin all, my country, you and hope !

HAROLD.

Thus will you make two lives most desolate,
And yet perhaps purchase no benefit,
Nor stay calamity.

EDITH.

Take not away
From my sad soul the only thing I gain
When I give all, the martyr's holy hope
When the flame wraps him, dying for his faith !

HAROLD.

Edith, beware of useless sacrifice !

EDITH.

Your love, alas ! tempts you to cruel words.

HAROLD.

To spare more cruel act.

EDITH.

     No, Harold, no;
I must not listen unto sophistry.
A last farewell—I shall not see you more,
But I will pray most constantly to Heaven
To send its blessings on you; so my love
Will be outpoured in prayer.

       Edith moves away.

HAROLD.

      Stay! Edith—stay!
 Edith stops, turns to him, makes a gesture of
  sorrowful refusal, then goes out.
She's gone! I am a plaything now for chance.
Calamity, thy sharpest sting is here;
I fear no more, so fatal this last stroke,
So crushed am I — Ill-chance hath wrought its worst;
And time hath nothing more to equal this—
My country—yes—
  Draws his sword, and kneels to make oath on the
   cross of its hilt.
     Here I devote my life
To make this sacrifice of worth to thee.

Edith, within her convent, yet shall hear
How Harold saved his land, or she will weep
When they bring tidings of his faithful death,
Fighting the Norman.   Take, ye bones of saints,
This oath in place of one I cannot keep.'

> *Bows down his head over the cross-hilts of his
> sword.*

ACT IV.

SCENE I.—LONDON.

Hall of state in the KING'S *palace.*

Guards and attendants.

FIRST ATTENDANT.

Think you the king will sit in state to-day?

SECOND ATTENDANT.

I have it from his Master of the Robes
He will.   Though very weak and deathly sick,
He hath a sick man's craving to be placed
Once more in state, so fitly to receive
From the Archbishop notice in due form
Of the high consecration of his church,
Westminster Abbey.

FIRST ATTENDANT.

       Why doth he hear it now,
So sick; not wait the time of better health?

SECOND ATTENDANT.

'Tis whispered that his health will not be better.
He vowed, long years ago, a pilgrimage
To Rome, which failing, he hath built this church,
His dispensation from the holy father,
And fain would see all finished ere he dies:
His mind so dwells upon it, he must rise
From his sick-bed for this important audience.
See, here he comes; how very weak he is!
Look how he leans upon the Earl.

FIRST ATTENDANT.

                              Yes—yes;
This audience is his last.

SECOND ATTENDANT.

                    Hush! take your place.

Enter the KING, *supported on one side by* EARL
HAROLD, *on the other by* ARCHBISHOP ALDRED;
*he is placed in his chair of state, and is accom-
panied by* EARLS GURTH *and* MORKAR, *thanes,
guards, and attendants.*

KING, *feebly.*

Tell the Archbishop of Canterbury we give
Him audience.

Attendants go out, and bring in ARCHBISHOP
STIGAND *and priests. The* KING *sinks back
in his chair as if unconscious;* HAROLD *bends
over him, then turns to* ARCHBISHOP STIGAND.

HAROLD.

My Lord, the king would hear
If you have made with fitting ceremony
The consecration of his church.

ARCHBISHOP STIGAND.

My liege,
Your gift to God, Westminster's lordly pile,
His servants have, with all accustomed rites,
Sealed to his service.   Your most holy vow
Unto Christ's vicar is by this discharged,
And in his name I now confirm to you
All the indulgence and your sins' remission
Beforetime promised by our holy father.
Such gifts of kings are pleasing in God's sight;
For, helping thus his church, you bring his light
Of love and saving to the hearts of men:
Thus as a king and servant of the Lord
You do a double service——He heeds me not !
My Lords, this stupor of the king is strange.

HAROLD.

Laying his hand on the KING'S *arm.*

My liege, the Archbishop brings you here the thanks
Of holy church for your most kingly gift.

KING.

Starting up and speaking wildly.

Yes, I am ready—look not on me so;
Your eyes, so deathly, fill me with affright:
I fear not death; but yet I fear your eyes.

HAROLD.

My liege, you dream, addressing empty space.
Who is it that you speak to? we see none.

KING.

That tall, dark palmer with the spectral eyes—
Nay, he is gone; bring him to me again,
For I would question him of this strange thing.

ARCHBISHOP ALDRED.

My liege, your sickness mounts into your brain:
There was no palmer here; it was a dream.

KING.

A strange dream, Lords. My soul, a premonition

That this your earthly life draws near an end.

Oh, take me, saints, to dwell with you in heaven!

God give me strength—if this thing comes of thee

And not of demons—to relate the story.

The vision, I have seen, came to me thus:

In Normandy, full forty years ago,—

I was young then, alas, how strange it seems!

Old now and sick,—a palmer came to me,

A strange, weird man with eyes that wildly gleamed

As if they looked on things most horrible.

He told me I should be a king, and rule

In England many, many troubled years;

That sin would flourish underneath my sceptre

Until God's vengeance shadowed all the land;

After my death, within a year and day,

My kingdom should be vanquished by a foe,

And all the land by demons overrun:

Then, when I asked him how to save the land,

He told me, "Nay, the land cannot be saved."

Departing, promised ere my life should cease

To come again, forewarning me of death.

This palmer, with his wild, unearthly eyes

Unchanged, nor looking older by a day

Than when I saw him forty years ago,

Stood here but now, and in a solemn voice

Spake thus to me: "King, I have come again

As I foretold; thou art, hast been a king,
And monstrous evils cumber all the land,
While over all a threatening shadow falls,
Still growing darker.   Death now draweth near
To claim you his; and afterward the land
And throne will pass by deed, red-writ in battle,
To a stranger, as I told you formerly.
Come, are you ready?"   Then I answered him;
And you spoke to me, Harold, and you, Aldred;
But when I looked again, the thing was gone.

ARCHBISHOP ALDRED.

I know not if this vision comes of God,
But take, O King, its warning, and prepare
To meet the saints.   But first one kingly act:
Name a successor to the English throne.
You have no son to be your lineal heir;
Who then shall have the rule?

KING.

Ah! who would be a king?   'Tis care and woe;
A happier lot the base-born peasant knows
Than is a king's—pain on his gold-bound brow.

HAROLD.

Dear liege, the Duke of Normandy, your cousin,

Claims England in the right of an old promise
From you to him; but England will be torn
With many wounds ere he can fill the throne.
Will you then leave such heritage of blood
Unto your kingdom? Be more wise, more kind;
Name a successor such that all may thank
And bless your name, you brought not here a stranger
To set his foot on England's liberties.

KING.

The crowning goodness of the King of Heaven
Calls me from this, my earthly throne, to kneel
Most humbly at his greater throne of grace.

ARCHBISHOP ALDRED.

Who leaves his duty unfulfilled on earth
Is not prepared to kneel before the throne
Of Him who portions duty unto all.
Give us your answer: Who shall be our king
When you give up this sceptre and your crown?

KING.

Son Harold, wouldst thou sit upon this throne,
And wear our majesty, and feel our woe?
A weary burden is the kingly robe.

HAROLD.

My gracious king, not for its majesty,
Name, office, power, will I sit on your throne;
My heart hath taken a deep, a mortal wound,
In which ambition died, and life's bright hopes;
So regal power hath lost its grace for me:
But what my country in its need requires,
That will I do; and if to wear a crown,
Not as a triumph, but as holy trust,
Its ring shall bind my brow. I do not seek it;
Its glitter tempts me not.

KING.

Take it, son Harold; none in all the land
So fit as you to rule. Ye ealdormen,
Take note: the king bequeaths his crown to Harold—
I cannot speak—this faintness grows on me.

   The KING *sinks back, and falls into a stupor.*

ARCHBISHOP ALDRED.

The king is very ill; it seems most fit
To bear him to his chamber; much I fear
He will not speak again.

KING.

  Starting to his feet, and speaking loudly.

    Ha! Sanguelac!

The lake of blood!—I see it, oh! I see it—
The army of the demons—Ha! and he
Who leads them on—I know those frightful eyes;
It is the palmer—no—he's clad in mail—
Duke William—Normans—demons—Help, O saints!
Help for the land!—Avaunt, ye dreadful spoilers!
The Lord hath bent his bow; it is his shaft—
My eyes are full of blood.   Help! help me! help!

> *The* KING *falls back into the arms of* HAROLD
> *and* ARCHBISHOP ALDRED.

ARCHBISHOP ALDRED.

A warning and a prophecy of ill.

ARCHBISHOP STIGAND.

Nay, do you fear the dreams of a sick man,
That thus you tremble, Lords, when fever flies
With its strange fancies through the dizzy brain
Painting fantastic, flitting images?

HAROLD.

Hush, priest! the king is dead.

> *Tableau.*

SCENE II.—LONDON.

Antechamber in the house of EARL HAROLD.

Enter MOLLO.

MOLLO.

Now must I think—what office will I have?
His chamberlain and treasurer is too high;
That's for a thane. The Master of the Robes?
That's not so easy. Or the Chief of Huntsmen?
Ah! that's too active. Something of profit, honor,
Nor yet too high. I must be always modest,
And make no enemies; for my wise head
Tells me the best philosophy is that
Which brings most comfort. Guthlac sighs for fame,
Longs for the battle like a neighing steed,
That he may capture Fortune; not so I;
If Fortune comes I'll shake her by the hand,
But never be so very impudent
To take by storm the maid. To try and miss
Would be misfortune, which men try to miss.
This household suits me well; perhaps the change,
Transforming our great earl into a king,

May spoil a good earl, make a so-so king;
But if he makes a good king or a bad,
Concerns me not so much as this one thing:
What doth it bring to Mollo? There's the risk.
Why should I seek for office when without it
I've been contented?—Why? Because of folly.
And I was thinking—stupid that I am—
To get an offiee—honor? profit?—no;
While here I eat the best, and drink the best,
Sleep on the softest down, am free from care.
How is my master, though they make him king,
Happier than I? his throne? his crown of pearl?
Who ever called King Edward happy king?
They called him saint and monk, sometimes blessed
       king,
But yet that blessing never happiness;
Who ever saw a smile upon his brow?
So should the witan, in their wisdom, choose
That I, instead of Harold, be their king,
I make my bow, I give them my best thanks,
But say, "My Lords, oh no; a king? not I;
I'd rather be a minstrel."   *Shouting without.*
          Ha, they come!

         PEOPLE, *without.*

Long live King Harold!
   F*   I

MOLLO.

     It is so ; they come
To bring the Earl dead Edward's shining fillet,
A pretty bauble glittering over cares.

PEOPLE, *without.*

Live England !　Saxon England and King Harold !

MOLLO.

They shout for England first ; that is themselves,
This noble people—   *Loud shouting.*
    Thing with many mouths ;
And all the mouths now stretched in noisy shouting.

PEOPLE, *without.*

Long live King Harold !　Long live Saxon England !

MOLLO.

A noisy people.　I'll go and be a mouth
To shout as loud as any.   *Exit leisurely*

SCENE III.—LONDON.

Hall in the house of EARL HAROLD.

EARL HAROLD, *sitting.*

There was a time when pure of heart and hand
I nursed ambition, not a wicked scheme
To rise by others' downfall, but a hope,
Rising to raise my country.   In that time
Of bright anticipations I looked forward
With delighted hope to the proud hour, now near,
When the great witan should declare me king,
Basileus of Britain.   Now,—how changed
By my own errors and false pride of judgment!
No hope springs up elastic in my heart
To shout with coming fortune; but I wait
Content in sadness to accept a duty.
                    Starts up impatiently.
If I could drive away the guilty Past,
Banish the haunting Future, call up Hope
Again to crown her with this majesty
And name her Edith—this were happiness,
And this the day I dreamed of long ago.

Impossible !
The bones of saints grin at me in derision.

Enter GUTHLAC.

GUTHLAC.

The chiefs of England come to greet their king.

Enter ARCHBISHOPS OF YORK *and* CANTERRURY,
EARLS GURTH *and* MORKAR, *thanes, etc.*

ARCHBISHOP ALDRED.

Harold, the witan chooseth you our king.
Though not of Cerdic's line, O son of Godwin,
We choose you for your faithful English heart ;
We choose you for your arm of Saxon strength ;
We choose you for your valiant Danish blood ;
We choose the soldier who knows not defeat ;
We choose the ruler who is always just ;
We choose the statesman, wise and politic.
Hail Harold, King of England !

ALL.

Hail Harold, King of England !

HAROLD.

And I, most holy fathers, earls and thanes,
Accept the trust you proffer to my hands,

A sacred trust from England and from God.

The sceptre I will hold with even hand ;

Do equal justice unto high and low ;

Sustain the law ; restrain all lawlessness ;

Build unto stronger union our dear land,

Making one brotherhood of Danes and Saxons ;

That England may rejoice in healthful strength,

And fair Prosperity, with lavish hand,

Pour wealth and plenty on our favored island.

So may I reign for no vain pageantries

Or idle pleasures, but my country's good ;

And God so judge me as I keep this pledge.

> HAROLD *sits.* GURTH *advances, kneels and places*
> *his hand on* HAROLD'S *knee.*

GURTH.

I choose you, Harold, for my lord and king.

> MORKAR *advances, kneels and places his hand*
> *on* HAROLD'S *knee.*

MORKAR.

I choose you, Harold, for my lord and king.

> *Thanes successively kneel and place their hands*
> *on* HAROLD'S *knee.*

THANES.

I choose you, Harold, for my lord and king.

ARCHBISHOP STIGAND.

My liege, your coronation should proceed
With all convenient speed ; we know not what
A day, an hour may bring.   Please you appoint
The time when all the rites of church and state
May join to consecrate our new-made king.

Enter OSBALD *hastily.*

OSBALD.

Earl Harold, news !

GURTH, *grasping* OSBALD'S *arm.*

Kneel, fellow, to your king.

OSBALD kneels, then rises.

OSBALD.

O King, defend your realm.   I come from York.
A mighty army is on Humber's banks ;
The river white with ships.   Tostig, the fierce,
And the Norwegian king, great Hardrada,
Lead on a wild, rapacious armament.
All Norway is afoot.   From casques of steel
Adown huge shoulders hangs their yellow hair,
As round a lion sweeps his tangled mane ;
They march, the fierce berserkers of the North,
With clash of shields, and shouting battle-songs,

While o'er them flap their frightful raven-flags.

O King, so great a peril never came;

So great an army never sought our shores,

Norwegian, Dane, in all the troubled past.

KING HAROLD.

They shall be met.   Go, Morkar, to your earldom;

Rouse all Northumberland, and lead their war

As once great Siward led; your brother, Edwin, ,

Must bring his Mercians.   Brave Gurth, your voice

And Leofwine's shall raise our Kent and Sussex;

Let our bold Saxons grasp the sword and axe

And come at Harold's call.   Ourself in person

Will levy here.   England shall leap to arms;

Make rough our shore with graves of slaughtered Norse.

Bishops, in haste I must be crowned to-night—

To-night in Westminster—if scant the rites.

The time brooks not delay—a king, full-crowned,

Must lead the embattled might of England forth

Against these fierce forayers of the North.

In all your churches ring the service bells,

Bid all your priests send up their solemn prayers

While our good swords cut down this heathen host.

Go each and act as if on him alone

His country's fate were hung.

                    Exeunt all but the KING.

Now beats my heart
As when it throbbed with sweet entrancing dreams :
If not for love, I live for England, glory.

Exit.

SCENE IV.—THE COUNTRY BEFORE YORK.

KING HARDRADA, TOSTIG *and soldiers.*

HARDRADA.

My friend, this town of York, is it not crazed?
It has no army ; burghers man its walls ;
If we let loose on it our dogs of war,
Their very howling will throw down its gates ;
And even now they strain upon the leash.
We may not hold them long.   Pray tell them this ;
If then they open not their gates to us
There will be wailing of their wives and daughters
When Norway storms their walls—what do they mean?

TOSTIG.

Most valiant Hardrada, our Englishmen
Have not been taught to yield ; they find it hard
To learn such lesson.   Give them time, my friend ;
Nor spoil the thing that surely will be ours.

HARDRADA.

They shall have time.　It is a goodly land,
This England, and we like it passing well;
We hear the king is sick; his idle throne,
Useless unto a sick man, waits for us;
And we will take it.　Is there any army
Or chief that dares to meet our Northern host,
To match his strength against King Hardrada?

TOSTIG.

The king is naught, but standing by his throne
Is Harold Godwinson, my father's son;
'Tis he will lead the army.　Dream not, King,
Harold will fly because your warriors shout;
Save all your strength; use all your boasted skill;
We shall need both when Harold brings us war.

HARDRADA.

My friend, we've lived and fought in many lands;
Faced the fierce Scythian, Saracen and Turk;
Met the wild horsemen of the Asian plains;
Fought in Caucasian mountains savage men
As rude as shaggy bears; but ne'er have seen
In any land such warriors as we bring
Into this war from Norway's stormy coasts.

Behold their brows, how wide; their eyes, how fierce;
Their shaggy hair, their stature huge and tall—
Each stands, a giant portraiture of Thor;
They'll kill and eat your stunted Englishmen.

TOSTIG.

Believe it not; I too have been a rover,
And looked on warriors of the East and North;
Our Englishmen fight well, I warn you, Hardrada.

HARDRADA.

See you yon clouds of dust? there are armed men;
I catch the glitter of their mail and arms
Emerging from the wood; it is a host.

TOSTIG.

I see them, King; look where yon banner flies—
Now, by Saint Swithin! as I truly think,
'Tis Harold leads the might of England hither.
Marshal your force; arrange your battle-lines;
You soon will see how Englishmen can fight.

HARDRADA.

Bring up my banner.   Plant the standard here.
Earl Tostig, ride with speed along our host
Upon the right; the left shall be my care;

Swing back the flank till like a crescent moon
Or reaper's sickle curves our gleaming line;
Thus we will gain this island-throne to-day,
Loosing our hungry ban-dogs in the land.

Exit HARDRADA.

TOSTIG.

Now will the Wolf's-head win his own again;
Or else—good-night to Tostig.

Exit.

SCENE V.—THE COUNTRY BEFORE YORK.

Another part of the field.

Enter SEXWULF, *armed with a Saxon boar-spear.*

SEXWULF.

No one sees me; now if I reach the wood
I shall be safe; but if they see and follow
It will be thought that I have fled from fear—
From fear?   What should I be afraid of?   Death?
A slave's life—humph! Wherefore should he save life?
For himself? no, he doth not own himself;
Then for his master?—fool, to take such trouble;

Yet, spite of reason, he defends his life
As if 'twere something that was worth his having.
Here is all England come to fight the Norsemen ;
Some fight for honor, lands, home, wife and children,
And the slaves fight because their masters bid them ;
But Sexwulf does not—lands, home, wife and children
He has not ; nor will fight when he is bidden.
Time was,—no—no ; why do I think of it ?—
When Sexwulf's children hung about his knees,
And his wife met him with a welcoming eye—
No—no ; I'll not remember it ; 'tis past :
A slave, what should he do with wife or children ?
And yet he had a heart to love, to hope,
To grieve, alas !   When they despoiled his home,
Robbed him of wife and children, Sexwulf wept ;
And, though a slave, suffered as suffer men.
Since then,—ah, many, many, weary years !—
No voice hath cheered him with kind word, save one
Whom Sexwulf followed as a dog, his master,
Content to be a slave because he loved ;
But him they killed—Cuthbert, my friend, my master,
Hunted to death by Tostig's savage band !
Now Sexwulf threatens Tostig—a slave, an earl.
How would this son of Godwin curl his lip,
His scornful lip, at a slave's enmity,
And kick me, like a dog, out of his lordly way,

Nor deign to turn his sharp sword's point on me,
Too good a death to give a base-born slave!
Cannot a slave then haply kill an earl?
Strip them of trappings, both are men alike;
Both built by Nature of her stuff for men.
I dare not face him—do I then lack courage?
No; armor, skill and weapons. I must lurk
Waiting for chance, that serves the base-born slave
As well as the great earl, to come behind,
And strike him through his armor. Ha, away!
I hear the clash of arms and tramp of feet—
How coward-like I fly from every sound,
Yet boast of killing earls!

> *Enter on one side* GUTHLAC, *on the other* KING
> HARDRADA, TOSTIG *and soldiers.* SEXWULF,
> *attempting to fly, is stopped by* TOSTIG.

Caught like a wolf-cub in a silly snare.

TOSTIG.

Speak; what art thou?

SEXWULF.

Sexwulf, the slave.

TOSTIG.

A slave—

What makes you here?

SEXWULF.

       They whipped me, and I fled ;
If I must fight, I'll fight against my country
Like great Earl Tostig, joined with Norway's ranks.

GUTHLAC, *aside.*

A cutting sarcasm, though the slave knows not
How sharp a sting he plants in Tostig's breast
Despite of sword-proof mail.

HARDRADA.

A sullen knave ; his welcome will be rude
Among our free-born warriors.

TOSTIG.

          Slave, begone !
                Exit SEXWULF.

Thane Guthlac, wherefore come you to our host ?

GUTHLAC.

A message to Earl Tostig from the king.

TOSTIG.

What king ? Here standeth one, King Hardrada,
Whose sword hath cut for him the golden round

Of sovereignty, nor yet hath dulled its edge.
What king?

GUTHLAC.

King Harold.

TOSTIG.

Is it so, indeed?
What have you done with Edward, that sweet saint?

GUTHLAC.

King Edward's dead.

HARDRADA.

Poor king.

TOSTIG.

Harold, a king!

HARDRADA.

'Twas not worth while; his reign will not be long.

TOSTIG.

What message to me from the King of England?

GUTHLAC.

King Harold sends his greeting to his brother:
He shall have peace, his friendship as of old
And all his ancient honors.

TOSTIG.

It is well;
The Wolf's-head asks no more.   What will he give
To my best friend and ally, Hardrada,
Who thus hath brought the Wolf's head back to grace?
What shall this warlike King of Norway have?

GUTHLAC.

A grave in England's soil.

HARDRADA.

`Ha! says he so?

TOSTIG.

Go back to Harold; give him this from me:
Tostig hath made his league with Norway's king,
And, come what may, he will abide the chance
To win or fall by brave Hardrada's side;
He should have sent me offers long ago;
It is too late to-day.

GUTHLAC.

King Hardrada,
Thus saith the King of England: quit the land,
You and your pirate horde, or he will sweep
All your Norwegian scum into the sea;
And Norway's widows, with lamenting wail,

Shall drown the roar of billows as they roll
In noisy tumult on your northern strands.

HARDRADA.

Tell your king this: Words fright not Hardrada,
Whose ear hath heard the Asian lion roar,
And the wild Tartars of the desert yell;
We come to fight.   Go back and tell him so.

Exeunt.

SCENE VI.—THE COUNTRY NEAR YORK.

The battle-field.   Alarums.   Enter KING HAROLD *and
soldiers.*

KING HAROLD.

Their lines are broken.   Far along the right
The gallant Leofwine rides down their host
With England's cavalry; upon the left
The men of Kent and Sussex, led by Gurth,
Have driven back their line.

Enter GURTH.

O my brave Gurth,
Thou art a warrior of the antique stamp!
How goes the day?

G   K   13

GURTH.

Brother, the day is ours;
King Hardrada is down, wounded or dead,
And all his Norsemen fly, while Leofwine
Tramples their host beneath his horsemen's feet :
It is a rout; to Stanford bridge they fly,
And o'er it to their ships.

Enter GUTHLAC.

KING HAROLD. ·

What news, good Guthlac?

GUTHLAC.

The day is ours; King Hardrada is slain—
A random arrow struck the Norway king,
And pierced his throat; he clutched and broke the
        shaft,
Gasped thrice, and died; I caught him when he fell,
And bade the soldiers bring his body here.

KING HAROLD.

He was the victor of a thousand fights;
His name is known on the far Caspian shores,
Along the Volga, by the Danube, Elbe,
And everywhere alike a conqueror;
Yet he comes here to die: thus slain by chance,

The random arrow he escaped so oft—
Why was he not content with Norway's throne?
Now all his land is but his length of earth.

Enter a soldier.

SOLDIER.

My liege, I come from Leofwine.   Our right
Now rests at Stanford bridge; o'er which in flight
Pours the Norwegian host, save those who lie,
Bleeding and dead, in piles along the way.

KING HAROLD.

Cannot brave Leofwine secure the bridge?
Why do we tarry with the field half won?

SOLDIER.

Before the bridge stands Tostig like a god,
And all go down before his gleaming sword;
Up to the bridge the Norsemen stragglers fly
From centre, right and left; he keeps his post,
While round him cluster a devoted band
On which our soldiers charge, but charge in vain;
Like Odin's self, he drives them fiercely back,
Still holds the bridge, and saves his flying host.
So Leofwine, who will not fight his brother,
Begs you to send a messenger of peace.

KING HAROLD.

Ill-fated Tostig, great amid defeat !
Guthlac, go you, and proffer from us peace ;
Peace unto him and all his flying host :
Tell him, good Guthlac, that his brothers' hearts
Are open to him still.   Come, friends, away ;
Gather our force ; the foe may turn again.

Exeunt.

SCENE VII.—BEFORE STANFORD BRIDGE.

Tostig, *leaning on his sword.*

TOSTIG.

Here ends the day ; the brave Hardrada slain,
And with him half his host ; the rest, dismayed,
Beyond the Derwent gather into bands
Marching toward their ships.   What now remains
For Tostig ?   Shall he join the flying host,
And purchase life with loss of name and honor ?—
Vanquished ! by Heaven, it galls me worse than death !—
A thing for scorn to mock at !   Men will say
" Hardrada won, if not the battle, glory,
Dying a soldier's death upon the field ;
But Tostig fled, as flies the frightened wolf,
His braver comrade slain."

Hardrada's death will give him deathless fame,
But Tostig's flight, a monument of shame.
Great King of Norway, your renown, death-bought,
Tostig will share; and when they tune their harps
To sing the valiant deeds of Sigurd's son,
One verse at least shall tell how Tostig fell,
More fearing shame than death.   They come again—
Ho! Norway! Norway!

TOSTIG *springs forward and meets* GUTHLAC *entering.*

GUTHLAC.

Nay, it is peace I bring.   Thus saith the king:
His former proffers doth he now renew,
Peace unto you and all the Norway host;
He offers you your place within his heart
And all your ancient honors in the land.

TOSTIG.

And doth he think I am so poor a thing
To creep up to his feet like a whipped dog?
He may give peace, but Tostig will not take it.
I stand at bay, though all my host be fled,
And still defy your England; I can die,
But will not yield, nor take your proffered peace—
No truce.   Strike, thane!

They fight. SEXWULF *enters, crouching at back,*
waiting an opportunity to strike TOSTIG.

13*

SEXWULF, *aside.*

I spy a broken link in Tostig's mail;
This is my chance to kill him.

> SEXWULF *advances and strikes his spear into*
> TOSTIG'S *back.* TOSTIG *turns and kills him;*
> *then leans heavily on his sword.*

TOSTIG.

Killed by a slave—at last to die a dog's death;
And I, an earl—Glory, I ever sought thee,
And thou hast baffled me at last—at last!
But none can say that Tostig ever feared;
He dies, like Danish jarl, with sword in hand,
And in his mail. Ah, Death, thy tooth is sharp;
It bites my heart; but I defy thee still!—
Ho, thane, strike on!

> TOSTIG *attempts to brandish his sword, but falls*
> *and dies.*

GUTHLAC.

Brave as a lion's, Tostig, was your heart,
But scarce less cruel than the king of beasts';
Your life ends here, but long will live your story
Brightening with valor's lustre evil deeds.   *Exit.*

ACT V.

SCENE I.—YORK.

A spacious hall. Soldiers banqueting KING HAROLD
sitting apart.

FIRST SOLDIER.

Drink, friends, the foaming ale, and thank your stars
You were not eaten by these Norway giants.

SECOND SOLDIER.

Giants indeed, man-eaters like enough;
For when I saw the huge Norwegians run,
It brought back to my mind that silly tale
Of childhood's wonder, him of the seven-leagued boots.

ALL. ·

Ha-ha!—ha-ha!

FIRST SOLDIER.

Old seven-leagued boots—that's good; but did you mark
What manes these Norsemen have?

THIRD SOLDIER.

Sea-lions' manes;

Yes, they have grown these shaggy fells of hair
In purpose of this visit, to affright us;
But, finding we remain unterrified,
Have back returned to grow them bigger manes.

SECOND SOLDIER.

But some will *re*mane here.

ALL.

Oh! oh!—ha-ha!

FIRST SOLDIER.

We'll drink a pleasant journey to them, friends;
Fill up the cups with ale.

ALL.

We drink to them.

KING HAROLD.

Life—a short day—an interval between
Nothing and darkness—flitting consciousness,
Vivid and startling as the lightning's flash;
And like that blinding glare beholding all,
But in an instant gone beyond recall.

Death—a grim phantom ever haunting Life—
The Night that swallows Day—a frightful pause—
The black reverse of Glory's shining shield—
Life's opposite, whose emblem is the grave.
Life, Death—the two conditions of one thing,
Whose margins meet ; which is the normal state ?
Which real, and which the shadow ?—which is health ?
And which disease ? to-day we have the one,
To-morrow comes the other—a slave's spear,
A random arrow, some disastrous chance,
And on this day of life, a black eclipse.
To him who dies, it is as if the world,
This solid, steadfast earth, on which is writ
Forever in its sunshine, at a touch
Melted again in chaos.   And what then ?
The future, grandly pictured by the church,
Is it a fact or fable? Let that pass.
O Tostig ! where thy valor now, thy strength,
Daring ambitions built above all hope?
Two days ago thou wast elate with life,
Now as inert and senseless as the sod
Cut by thy heels' sharp track.
And I must meet my mother ; her last words,
" Harold, be merciful unto my son,"
Ring in my ears ; but louder than her words
Fate called to him.   He fell, as falls a star—

G*

Across the heavens a bright and gleaming track,
Then quenched its light forever.   So to me,
My soul forewarns, will come the shaft of death.
         The sound of laughter is heard.
My thoughts suit not this revelry.   Thy ghost,
My brother, seems to sit in joyless gloom
Among these feasters, and my ear, intent,
Listens to catch thy tones.   Ho ! bring me wine.
              Enter EARL GURTH.
Your brow, my brother, wears no festive smile ;
Why do you slight the feast ?

GURTH.

                     Harold, my heart
Would not rejoice, nor fill with gayety.
Despite my knowledge of his fatal end
I looked for Tostig in each feaster's face,
Listened to hear his voice in every sound,
And, thus disturbed, could find no comfort here,
But sought the night-air's pure, refreshing breath
To cool the fever burning on my brow.

KING HAROLD.

Your words reflect the image of my thoughts ;
My mind, as yours, dear Gurth, is tortured still
With his remembrance.   Did the night-air calm

Your fevered pulse? dissolve the cloudy spell
Of the enchanter, Memory?

GURTH.

> Not so;
Too still the night: its solemn quiet thrills,
Not calms me. High in mid-heaven the moon shines full,
But pale her beams, and pale the stars peep out;
For in the northern sky, blood-red and bright,
Flashes our frightful visitant. Methought,
As on that red usurper of the night
I fixed my eyes, it threatened from the sky
Some strange calamity, more dread, alas!
Than this at which we groan.

KING HAROLD.

> It is enough
That this red comet sets its fatal sign
Upon the heavens to mark our brother's death,
Or shines, the doom-star of King Hardrada:
What should it more?

GURTH.

> Harold, I know not what;
But when I look upon that lurid star
With its broad trail of fire, thus making pale
Night's gleaming lights, and flouting the calm moon,

I feel a threat of yet impending ill.
Brother, do you remember Edward's dying cry
Of Sanguelac?
The fiery star repeats in every ray
That warning cry to my unquiet soul.

Enter a Messenger in haste.

MESSENGER.

O King, the Normans are on Sussex' shore—
Duke William and his host—as numberless
As are the stars in heaven or the sea-sands.

KING HAROLD.

This is the peril that the star portends.
O Gurth, my soul, prophetic as the star,
Hath looked each hour for this. Now, shadows, fly;
The certain presence of the direful fact
Scatters your phantoms, fills my heart with strength!
Where did the Norman land?

MESSENGER.

At Pevensey,
My Lord, he disembarked; the archers first,
Then knights and men in mail poured from his ships
Till the wide sands glittered with shining steel,
As when, a light breeze ruffling its broad breast,
The ocean shines with gleam of myriad waves.

KING HAROLD.

Do they bring horse, or are the knights afoot?

MESSENGER.

So many steeds were never seen before ;
Their neighing sounds tumultuous o'er the sands.

KING HAROLD.

Give o'er the feast ; muster our host to arms ;
We march to-night ; and the red comet's blaze
Shall light us on our way.   As Norway fell,
So shall the Norman.   No abiding-place
Hath England for the invader but a grave.

Exeunt.

SCENE II.—WALTHAM ABBEY.

The chapel.

Enter EDITH, *and kneels before an image of the Virgin.*

EDITH.

O virgin-mother of Christ crucified,
Heal the deep wounds that bleed continual here ;
Thou wast a woman, and once loved perchance—
Oh, pity me, and still my beating heart !

14

Rises.

I cannot pray as the calm sisters pray
With naught but pure devotion in their souls;
My prayers come all too fiery, and offend
This holy place with wild, impassioned thoughts.
Where is the comfort promised to my breast
In tranquil cloister-walls?   I find it not;
But a tumultuous conflict raging here
Beyond my power to quell; no comfort; pain—
A fever burning ever in my blood—
Strange phantasms in my brain; for oftentimes
I see weird figures round me, staring eyes
That look on me with cold, unaltering gaze,
Seeming so real, they fright me; but anon
They fade away, dissolving like a dream;
And then I know these phantoms have their life
In the hot brain of fever.   Why, alas!
May I not feel the calm and still content
Of duty done so loyally and wisely?—
Wisely?   Yes—yes; to think it was not wise
To give him up, were madness, now 'tis done.
They told me there would come a holy peace
Here in my heart when I was wed to Heaven—
Why comes it not? why must I think of him,
When now to think is sin?   I strive to pray,
But mid my prayers comes up his kingly face,

And his upbraiding eyes are fixed on me
Till prayers are changed to deep, heart-heaving sighs.
Why can I not forget?   These walls are cold;
The marble floor is chill; but yet I burn.
Oh, would that I were cold as this cold stone,
As senseless too!   I must still think of him.

Enter the ABBESS.

ABBESS.

Prayest thou, sister Edith, for our land
And those who fight against the heathen host,
Blind worshipers of Odin and of Thor?

EDITH.

I pray for peace.

ABBESS.

Pray to the saints, my child,
That all the land may have such holy peace
As clothes us, sisters, in these cloisters sweet.

EDITH.

Mother, to duty I have yielded me,
But peace comes not; I pray for it in vain.

ABBESS.

No peace in your pure heart—child, why is this?

EDITH.

I am not pure; I cannot tear my thoughts
From the remembrance of the world I've left.

ABBESS.

Pray—pray, my child; 'tis prayer that cureth all—

Enter a priest in haste.

Why do you come in such unseemly haste?

PRIEST.

The Archbishop bids you and your holy nuns
Send up your prayers to Heaven's high throne of grace
To shield the land from peril most extreme.
From Normandy a vast, Philistine host
Hath come upon our shores; the king in haste
Hurries to Sussex with the wearied bands
Which late he led in battle with fierce Norway;
Spent with sore marches and the recent battle,
His army is much wasted.　Pray, O nuns,
For never yet came peril to our land
So great as this; except the angels fight
Upon our side, there is no hope of help
For England else.　Then raise your solemn prayers,
O holy nuns, your supplications make
To Heaven's benignant saints.

ABBESS.

Alas, alas, that man should still slay man!
Go, priest, and bid them ring the Abbey bells;
I haste to call our sisters unto prayer.

Exeunt ABBESS *and priest.*

EDITH.

What said the priest?—Harold is on his march
To meet a great Philistine host from Normandy,
And England needs the prayers of priest and nun
In her great peril? Oh, away, black doubts!
Why do you come, with whispers in my ears,
Foretelling Harold's death? Alas, my soul,
This is a shadow blacker than the night
Surrounding you!—his death—I cannot rest;
I cannot pray; I think alone of Harold;
I feel his doom here in my poor, lone breast
That once was gay with happy love for him—
Still do I sin, a nun, to think of love;
I still remember when I should forget.
O Harold, if I could but see you once,
Once more ere death shall join or sunder us,
I might die happy! why should I stay here?
They told me peace would come, and it comes not.
I know that I must die; why may I not
Look once again on Harold ere I die?

L   14*

If it be sin, I cannot help but sin,
For I must think of him—Yes, I will go
While now confusion so disturbs the Abbey
That none will think of me.

> *Kneels at the crucifix.*

I sought for peace
Here at thy feet, O holy Son of Him
Who made all human hearts, all woes, all pains
And life for sacrifice ; but found it not :
Then pardon if I wander forth alone
To look upon his face again and die !

> *Kisses the crucifix.*

Pardon—oh, pardon for this last, great sin !

> EDITH *lays down her head at the foot of the crucifix.*

SCENE III.—SENLAC.

The camp of the English—before the king's tent. Evening. Soldiers and HUGH MARGOT. *Enter the* KING, EARL GURTH, *and* ARCHBISHOPS *of* YORK *and* CANTERBURY.

SOLDIER *to* HUGH MARGOT.

Kneel to the king.

MARGOT.

         Soldier, unto no king,
Except the King of heaven, Hugh Margot kneels.
I come to Harold from the Norman camp;
Thus saith Duke William: "To fair Normandy
Earl Harold came as guest, and swore an oath
At Edward's death to be Duke William's man,
And place him on this throne.   The Duke hath come
To take his throne; let Harold give the help
That he hath sworn."

KING HAROLD.

            Go tell the wolf, your master,
Although his scheme goes on, and you have brought
This, my denial, as he looks to have it,
A Saxon king awaits him sword in hand;
So let him cast away the fox's hide
Whose mask hath served his purpose long enough,
And come with wolfish visage plain in view
To take the advantage that his craft hath won.
Of broken oaths, say this to him: in his trap
Was Harold caught, and took to save himself—
A lawful means when life thus stands in peril—
Such oath as was prescribed; that oath the church
Hath since annulled; 'twas void, because compelled,
Without the help of church; nor rests with Harold

The power to give away this island crown;
'Tis not a thing to toss from hand to hand,
But rests securely fixed upon his head
The witan chooseth.

MARGOT.

These are empty words;
I come not here to learn your country's laws,
But to demand of you in William's name
Your solemn oath and this your stolen crown.

KING HAROLD.

Insolent priest! but for your gown and cowl
You should be scourged back to the Norman camp.
We do refuse; he shall not have the crown
Till from these shoulders he hath hacked the head,
And plucked its circle from a dead king's helm.

MARGOT.

The Duke, anticipating such deceit
And the perfidious voiding of your oath,
Gives this last choice: first, to retain the crown,
His greatest vassal; second, to the Pope
Refer your cause; or third, the high appeal
To Heaven by single battle with the Duke.

KING HAROLD.

Our cause we leave with Heaven, but will not stand
Like one accused of crime to champion it
With single might; nor wear a vassal crown;
Nor bow us to the policy of Rome:
But at the head of England's loyal hearts
Will meet the Duke.   If God will have it so,
Then William may be king; but not until
King Death hath made a subject of King Harold.

MARGOT.

Thus ends my mission from the Norman Duke:
He sends you his defiance, and will come
With sword and spear to take your crown to-morrow.
Now stand I forth the chosen messenger
Of one more high than he.   Pope Alexander
Sends thus to Harold: keep your sacred oath,
Sworn upon holy relics of the saints,
With due obedience as a hallowed thing,
The which to break, were foulest sacrilege,
Rank disobedience to the church and God,
Or on your guilty head he bids me place
The anathema of church—

ARCHBISHOP ALDRED.

> Priest, stay your words;

His holiness knows not that this rash oath
Hath been absolved by church, due penance paid,
And thus the sin atoned.

MARGOT.

And who art thou,
A bishop to oppose the head of church,
To cast contempt upon the holy saints,
To absolve the vows upon their relics sworn
Without due sanction and the seal of Rome?—
Thy act is void; it doth recoil on thee;
Beware! for so thou shar'st with him the doom
Pronounced by Rome.

To KING HAROLD.

If from this hour you dare,
O Harold, wage with Heaven an impious war,
Upon such act is set a curse, whose blight
Will wither up your crown as perisheth
A leaf in autumn, or some useless scroll
Lapped by red tongues of hungry furnace flames.
Nor you alone, but all who hold with you,
Friends, kindred—yea, the realm that calls you king—

KING HAROLD.

Now, by Saint Swithin! priest, you pluck the stars
Upon your head.—My guards.—Unless immortal,

Call on Saint Peter; you will need his help
To draw your cowled head from the lion's jaws.
 Soldiers come forward and surround HUGH MARGOT.
Strip off this caitiff's gown.

MARGOT.

     What will you do?

KING HAROLD.

Hang you upon a tree, and send your ears
To your two masters.
     GURTH.

    Brother, it is a priest,
And you, a king.   'Twould sully you to harm him.
Let him go free; he is beneath your anger.
Your kingly scorn will carry shame to them
That stooped so low to send this creature hither
With base attack upon your majesty;
Another snare by crafty cunning set.

KING HAROLD, *to soldiers.*

Take him away, and thrust him from our lines.

MARGOT.

Saint Peter's help!—
    GURTH.

    Silence, audacious priest.
 Soldiers take away HUGH MARGOT.

ARCHBISHOP STIGAND.

Thus Rome, allied with William, lends its strength
To the invader's arm; but Rome is not the church.

ARCHBISHOP ALDRED.

That is, or not, as William wins or fails:
He is the new apostle, with whose sword
May yet be writ the mandates of the church.

KING HAROLD.

They tell me, bishops, in the Norman host
Odo, the Bishop of Bayeux, in mail
Will lead Duke William's iron cavalry;
What say you: may we strike a bishop's helm?

ARCHBISHOP ALDRED.

Yes, when the helmet hides the mitred cap.

GURTH.

My liege, both as a liegeman and a brother
I offer counsel, which I pray you heed;
For in my voice the heart of England speaks,
Your army and your nation. Leave this field;
Return to London; levy there fresh troops
To fight, if Senlac's lost, another field;
Leave, my dear king, to-morrow's fate with me.

Your practiced eye hath marked these marshaled lines
Stretched far beyond our own.   Who knows the end?
If Heaven and Fate decree to-morrow's sun
Shall shine on victor William, let that sun
Still gild the evening with a ray of hope,
Not set on England, kingless.   Senlac lost,
Around the king will rally English hearts,
And Norman victory bind William's brows
With thorny chaplet, not with England's crown ;
For still before his march will armies spring,
As sprang to life in Greece the dragon's teeth—
And fighting men are England's dragon's teeth.
So may you save our land, whatever chance
Falls on this field of Senlac ; but your death
Will give our country to the Norman's sword ;
Nor Danish valor, nor our Saxon strength,
Avail for aught but sacrifice of life.

ARCHBISHOP ALDRED.

My liege, I think your brother's counsel wise ;
Hazard not all upon to-morrow's chance.

ARCHBISHOP STIGAND.

My counsel joins with Aldred's and brave Gurth's.

KING HAROLD.

No.   Though there seems a specious policy
In such advice, 'tis a deceitful seeming.

H   15

Shall England's king be first to fly the field,
Setting such base example? 'Twere enough
To throw disheartenment upon our host;
And every Saxon cheek within our lines—
Yes, in all England from the sea to sea—
Would burn with shame to hear of such a flight.
Bishops, when on my head you placed the crown
I swore my arm should smite the invader's helm:
Thus you would have me break another oath,
That men may point at me in holy scorn,
And name me the Oath-breaker—I, who sought
To add to Godwin's name a greater glory,
Thus tarnish all the honors of the past.
Brave Gurth, I know the greatness of your heart,
How bravely you would go to death for me,
Would fight this battle against any odds—
It must not be; Senlac to me is fate:
So speak no more of flight.

GURTH.

One reason more:
Harold, although your oath was plucked from you
By shameful fraud, yet it was greatly sworn;
And on it rests Duke William's strongest claim
Before the world and church. The church hath sent
Rome's gonfanon, Saint Peter's priest-blessed flag,
Beneath whose folds the Norman robber stands;

All this machinery of subtle Rome
Were forceless, if arrayed against our land,
Not Harold.   Though in Heaven's clear-seeing view
His heart is spotless, yet in eyes of men,
Whose ears have been deceived by crafty tales,
Our king is branded with a perjury,
So stamped by the pontifical seal of Rome.

KING HAROLD.

Still more the reason that I keep the field;
To fly were to confess my oath yet binds,
And strengthen William's fraud.   Our cause is just:
For Saxon liberty we stand arrayed
As stood three-hundred at Thermopylæ
Against rapacity and robber-greed;
If with the robber now is joined the church,
Upon the church must fall the deep disgrace
Of such alliance; and all honest hearts
Are thus absolved from use of ancient homage.
The church was made for man, to lift his soul
By prayer and precept to the light of heaven;
While thus it elevates, our duty, love
And calm obedience are its rightful dues;
But when ambition mounts Saint Peter's chair
To hold a temporal sceptre over men,
Dimming the native light within their souls,
And making superstition the false coin

With which to purchase power and luxury,
Then doth a demon take the apostle's place,
And grin sardonic o'er obedience blind.
If aught descended from our sires of old
Is dear, that heritage is liberty;
And who would rob us of our ancient rights
An enemy, whatever garb he wear,—
Whether he come clad in the Norman's steel,
Or with black gown, shorn head and sandaled foot.

Enter GUTHLAC.

My faithful thane, what of Earl Morkar's force?

GUTHLAC.

It stays at London still, for some equipments,
Full ranks, for certain chiefs, for this and that.
I told the Earl your need, urged instant march:
He put me off a while; but, when I clamored,
Bade me go forward and report his march
Within three days.

KING HAROLD.

        Within three days! O Fate,
Whate'er thou hast for England, woe or weal,
Concealed in thy dark bosom, shall be known
When sinks to-morrow's sun!—We cannot wait
For tardy Morkar. Were old Siward living,
Here had he stood, and, ready at his call,

Around us had been camped Northumbria.
Well, be it as it is.   My friends, to rest:
At dawn the Norman will attack our lines;
Our plan of battle is to hold these heights,
And keep compact and close our firm array,
Which, like a wedge, stretches along the hill.
We need not fear the Norman cavalry
While we can keep our lines; I've fought in France,
And know their horse will not ride down the spears.
Good-night: to which may come a happy morrow.

Exeunt all but the KING *and* GURTH.

Gurth, should the Norman still delay attack,
And Morkar come, the chance would count for us.
No one, like you, can urge his tardy steps
To quicker motion; you must ride to-night,
And bring this brother-in-law of ours along;
I give you but two days.

GURTH.

Two days too much.
I will not quit the field, let Morkar come
Or stay; after to-morrow is too late.
Brother, good-night.

KING HAROLD.
Good-night.

They clasp hands, then part, but turn again.

GURTH.

My brother!

KING HAROLD.

Brother!

They embrace tenderly.   *Exeunt.*

SCENE IV.—SENLAC.

Within the English lines. Morning.

Alarums. Enter MOLLO, armed, and soldiers.

MOLLO.

I grow to greater valor every hour;
It only needs the practice of the field
To be a hero. When the Normans charged
I felt a something tempting me to run,
But shut my eyes, and manfully kept place
Fast in the ranks: now, my first tremblings over,
And it is said all men feel fear at first,
I am as brave as Arthur. Practice—practice—
It makes the hero, poet, minstrel, statesman.
Though inclination did not bring me here,
Yet, being here, in faith I'll win a garland
       Arrows fall about him.

Only these flying arrows set me back.
If one should hit? Saint Cuthbert! where were Mollo?
Instead of garland I may get an arrow;
I'll try make shift to do without them both.

Loud cries and alarums.

Lo! all the Normans now have turned their backs—

To the soldiers.

Down on them, soldiers; give them hot pursuit;
Come, friends.

Cries of Holy Rood, and clash of arms.

FIRST SOLDIER.

Our orders are to keep the lines.

MOLLO.

To keep the lines!   how may we win a battle
If we shall keep the lines?

SECOND SOLDIER.

That's very true.

FIRST SOLDIER.

The time to charge is when the word is given;
'Tis the young soldier's fault to be in haste:
I followed our brave king, when he was earl,
Through the Welsh wars, and know the rules of service.

MOLLO.

See how our comrades break their ranks, and charge;
If we stay longer we shall stay alone.

SECOND SOLDIER.

See how they strike the Normans; let us go.

FIRST SOLDIER.

I like not this; and doubt it will end well.

MOLLO.

We stay too long—cry Holy Rood, and charge.

> MOLLO *and soldiers charge, crying England!*
> *Holy Rood!*

SCENE V.—ON THE HIGH GROUND BEHIND THE FIELD OF SENLAC.

Saxon women kneeling at a stone cross. On the left,
ARCHBISHOPS ALDRED *and* STIGAND *and priests;*
on the right, EDITH, *her face covered with her black*
nun's hood.

ARCHBISHOP ALDRED.

The Saxon line no longer crowns the ridge;
I miss the glitter of its shields and spears;

They have descended on the Norman host;
Pray God they drive it to the sea.

ARCHBISHOP STIGAND.

　　　　　　　　Amen.
Yet 'twere a miracle; I dare not hope it.

ARCHBISHOP ALDRED.

Although the Norman host outnumber ours
Threefold, yet number is but an element
In this great problem of a nation's fate.

ARCHBISHOP STIGAND.

Yonder is worked the fate of men, not nations:
King Harold vanquished, slain, the wrath of Rome
Against the perjurer is quenched by death;
The Pope withdraws Saint Peter's gonfanon;
Duke William fights the Ætheling's adherents,
And in the end right vanquisheth the wrong:
The rightful king shall sit on England's throne.

ARCHBISHOP ALDRED.

Short-sighted man! see you no more than this?
Mark me: behind yon ridge that bars our sight
Rome fights for empire over all the land;
William and Normandy are but the tools

4*　　　　M

Of an ambition, to the which their own
Is a faint mimicry.   These fight for self,
Lucre, estates, place, luxury and greed;
Rome fights for rule over the human mind,
An intellectual throne, on which may sit
Her pontiff, and direct the subject world
As Latin Jove upon Olympus sat.
Brother, the men are playthings of the hour,
They rise and fall as Fortune's wheel goes round;
But o'er mankind moves on a larger wheel,
Developing from embryos in the present—
Men and their puny acts—the future's fate.
On Harold's helm sits Saxon liberty,
The dearest right of man—to be a man—
Himself the pilot of his voyage of life.
Pray for it, priest, or live to mourn its loss.

Enter a priest.

How goes the field?

PRIEST.

Alas! no longer well.
When first the Norman stormed the English line,
Down went his ranks beneath the Saxon axe,
And everywhere repelled were driven back
With much confusion, disarray and loss;
Again and still again, with lines reformed,

Duke William led them on, still to recoil
From the long swing of the great Saxon axe;
But ever, bringing death upon their points,
Fell on our lines the Norman archers' shafts.
As stinging wasps drive the slow ox to frenzy,
So our men
Were driven at last by this fast-falling death
To break their ranks, and follow on the foe
As he once more recoiled.
A fatal charge, for which throughout the day
The Norman Duke had watched; he gave the word;
On came his horsemen, met our broken lines,
And rode them down.   Then Gurth and Leofwine
Sought to bring back this van into the ranks
Of those who stayed fast by the palisades.
Our two brave Earls charged through the struggling mass
Till down before them on the bloody field
Fell the great Duke and his bold bishop-brother,
To whose quick rescue came a thousand knights
And sore beset the Earls.
Then charged King Harold with a chosen few
Deep in the mingled ranks that closed on him
As closes ocean on the tribute flood
A rapid river gives the gulping sea.
Upon the English heights all hearts were hushed
In dread anxiety to know the fate

Of half the host and their heroic king.
At length, by dint of prowess, from the mass
Of mingled combatants and flashing arms,
As breaks the moon through black and stormy clouds,
Won back the sons of Godwin with a part,
A little part, of all
Who left their station on the guarded heights.
But when I left the field the Norman host
Had charged again, and on the left broke through
The weakened lines; the chance is now against us.

ARCHBISHOP ALDRED.

How fares the king?

  EDITH *presses forward, and lifts the hood from her face in great eagerness to hear the answer.*

PRIEST.

    King Harold fights on foot
In the front rank where danger presseth most;
The valor and the might of his brave line
Show on his kingly front.   Before his axe
Go down the Normans as a field of corn
Falls by the reaper's steel; no Norman knight
Hath crossed his path and come unharmed away.
The soldiers catch an inspiration from him,
Send loud along their line his battle-cry

Of " England I Holy Crosse !" upon his helm
Glitters the golden circle of a king;
The mark of many arrows, harmed by none,
He strides through perils as his life were charmed,
And seems the guardian god of England's realm.

ARCHBISHOP ALDRED.

O holy saints, shield him for England's sake!

EDITH, *touching her head.*

Alas ! I cannot think ; I see and hear,
But in my brain a roaring like the sea
That deafens thought, while something whispers me,—
A startling, frighting whisper, clearly heard
Through all the tumult of my dizzy head,—
To-night—to-night—to-night.

Exeunt.

SCENE VI.—THE BATTLE-FIELD.

Under the king's standard.   Evening.   Enter KING
    HAROLD *and* EARL GURTH, *meeting; their armor
    defaced and bloody.*

KING HAROLD.

England is lost I O Gurth, our England's lost !

GURTH.

This field of Senlac is not England, Harold.
You have done all a valiant king can do
Giving the invader battle on the shore;
Duty now calls you to collect again
The men of England; let each rising ground,
Each river-bank, be made a battle-field,
On which the Norman must fight o'er this day.

KING HAROLD.

It is in vain.   At me misfortune points.
All England bears calamity for me;
Takes it at second-hand because of me.
All I have left to give my country now
Is the example of a kingly death;
That service Fate is powerless to prevent.
From hollow skulls the pitiless saints mock at me,
While by their fleshless arms is England scourged,
Aiming at me.   I can at least end this;
By death at once avert from my dear land
Their angry blows.   I owe my country this.

GURTH.

My brother and my king, this gloomy day
Hath so disheartened your heroic soul
Your wisdom falters too.

KING HAROLD.

              What is there left?
This ridge of hill is piled with Saxons slain;
England's brave sons were faithful even to death:
Here lie the men of Sussex, Wessex, Kent,
Anglia and Mercia—all stout hearts; no foot
Would fly, no hand relax its grasp of sword
Or axe—see how they gripe in their dead hands
Their weapons. Gurth, I led them to this field;
I set them here, the prey of greedy death;
If, for I am accursed, these men have died,
What frightful punishment for broken oaths!

GURTH.

This is not so; they fought as through the past
Their sires have met Norwegian, Celt, or Dane,
Whatever foe has landed on our shores;
They died, as died their sires, defending England.

KING HAROLD.

O Gurth, I am accursed; they died for me!

GURTH.

No more for you tnan for all Englishmen.

KING HAROLD.

I sought to serve thee, England, but, alas !
I have destroyed thee !
So I am guilty, guiltless of this blood—
Here's my last stand ;
Here, underneath my warrior-flag, I stay ;
For, if I cannot conquer, I can die.

GURTH.

A useless sacrifice.   The field is lost ;
Then husband life to fight a fairer field.

KING HAROLD.

Shall Tostig show more valor in his end,
Or Hardrada, the champion of the North,
Who paid the forfeit of defeat with death,
Than I?   O Gurth, 'twere base in me, a king,
To fly the field where I have led to death
The bravest and the best of all the land.
How could I meet our mother, leaving here
On this sad field my brother Leofwine,
His smiling brow defaced by bloody death ?
No—no ; the only kingly act now left,
The fitting end of my disastrous reign,
Brave death ; so will a golden lustre gild
Through black calamities my fatal crown.

To your brave conduct I bequeath the war ;
No frowning saints will mutter round your head ;
Your hands are clean and strong—dear Gurth, farewell.

GURTH.

I am enamored too of glorious Death.

KING HAROLD.

Both as your king and as your elder brother
I bid you leave me—for our mother's sake—
Leave her at least one son.

GURTH.

    When I shall say,
"I left King Harold on the field of Senlac
To fight alone beneath his warrior-flag,"
What welcome will she give me?

KING HAROLD.

Bravest of men and faithfulest of brothers !—
Despair, make room within my heart for love ;
A brother's love disputes the place with you,
And gilds departing life with rosy tints !
  KING HAROLD *and* GURTH *embrace.*
This soil of Sussex was our cradle, Gurth,

16*

And here must be our grave ; but Godwin's sons
Shall live in story, if, in Saxon England,
Survives the legend of her liberty.

Alarums.

GURTH.

Come, brother, come,
And charge the Normans—two against a host.

KING HAROLD.

England and Edith, take my last farewell.
Ho ! England ! England ! Holy Crosse !

Alarums.

KING HAROLD *and* GURTH *charge.*

SCENE VII.—THE BATTLE-FIELD.

Night.   The bodies of the slain lying under the light
of the stars.   Enter two priests with torches, and
EDITH *searching among the corpses of the slain for*
that of KING HAROLD.

FIRST PRIEST.

Brother, in pity shall we still go on,
Or take her hence ?

SECOND PRIEST.

In her insanity

Perhaps she would not know King Harold's body

If chance should bring her to it.

FIRST PRIEST.

I think she would.

SECOND PRIEST.

See here what piles of slain ; here died at bay

Some mighty English hearts.   How ghastly seems

Death on the battle-field ! no glory gilds

These mangled ones ; yet here perhaps they died

As gloriously as Curtius when he leaped

Into the yawning chasm.   Here they fought on,

Hopeless of victory or saving life,

No eye to mark their valor, and no tongue

To tell how gloriously they fell—

EDITH *raises the head of the dead king.*

EDITH.

Light ! light !—

'Tis he ! 'tis he !   Mine—mine at last !—mine now

And to eternity !   Death, thou art feared

As one who bringeth sorrow ; but to me

Thou bring'st a bridegroom and eternal joy !

O Harold !—Harold !—Harold !

EDITH *falls on the body of* KING HAROLD.

FIRST PRIEST.

Unloose her hands—I think it is the king.

SECOND PRIEST.

'Tis he indeed.

They unclasp EDITH'S *arms from the dead king,
and raise her up.*

She faints.

FIRST PRIEST.

She's dead.

SECOND PRIEST.

So soon?

God give her poor, crazed mind the sweet of rest.

FIRST PRIEST.

Amen.

Tableau.

THE END.

CPSIA information can be obtained
at www.ICGtesting.com
Printed in the USA
LVOW13s0350120818
586687LV00011B/801/P